How not to worry

How not to worry

Caroline Carr

Viva Books

New Delhi | Mumbai | Chennai | Kolkata | Bangalore | Hyderabad | Kochi | Guwahati

First Indian Edition 2010

VIVA BOOKS PRIVATE LIMITED

- 4737/23 Ansari Road, Daryaganj, New Delhi 110 002
  E-mail: vivadelhi@vivagroupindia.net, Tel. 42242200
- 76, Service Industries, Shirvane, Sector 1, Nerul, Navi Mumbai 400 706
  E-mail: vivamumbai@vivagroupindia.net, Tel. 27721273, 27721274
- Jamals Fazal Chambers, 26 Greams Road, Chennai 600 006
  E-mail: vivachennai@vivagroupindia.net, Tel. 28290304, 28294241
- B-103, Jindal Towers, 21/1A/3 Darga Road, Kolkata 700 017
  E-mail: vivakolkata@vivagroupindia.net, Tel. 22836381, 22816713
- 7, Sovereign Park Apartments, 56-58, K. R. Road, Basavanagudi, Bangalore 560 004
  E-mail: vivabangalore@vivagroupindia.net, Tel. 26607409, 26607410
- 101-102 Mughal Marc Apartments, 3-4-637 to 641, Narayanguda, Hyderabad 500 029
  E-mail: vivahyderabad@vivagroupindia.net, Tel. 27564481, 27564482
- Beevi Towers, First Floor, SRM Road, Kaloor, Kochi 682 018, Kerala
  E-mail: vivakochi@vivagroupindia.net, Tel: 0484-2403055, 2403056
- 232, GNB Road, Beside UCO Bank, Silpukhuri, Guwahati 781 003
  E-mail: vivaguwahati@vivagroupindia.net, Tel: 0361-2666386

www.vivagroupindia.com

Published by arrangement with

Crimson Publishing,
a division of Crimson Business Ltd
Westminster House, Kew Road
Richmond, Surrey TW9 2ND

ISBN : 978-81-309-1520-3

Published by Vinod Vasishtha for Viva Books Private Limited, 4737/23, Ansari Road, Daryaganj, New Delhi - 110 002.

Printed and bound by Raj Press, R-3, Inderpuri, New Delhi - 110 012.

Acknowledgements

With love and respect to ND, EG, and GL

Thank you so much to everyone who has contributed to this book. I am so grateful to those of you who shared your personal experiences, and to the professionals who gave me so much help and advice.

Contents

Introduction

If you or someone you know is over-anxious, worried and fearful, this book will be your best friend.

You may be desperate for answers to these questions:

- What is happening to me?
- Why have I got this?
- Will I always feel like this – will it ever go away?

Those that love you will want answers to these questions too. They will also want to know what they can do to help.

This book will help you, whatever your level of worry. It will also be useful if you live with someone who worries too much, because it will offer some tips on how to help them, and how to look after yourself too.

The ideas and tips in this book have all been tried and tested by real people. Some may work better for you than others – and that's fine. All the case studies given are real, though of course the names have been changed.

Some of the ideas will suggest that you use your imagination, or that you visualise something. If you are one of the many people who doesn't actually 'see' something in your mind's eye – that is fine. Perhaps you just 'know' instead. So just do it in whatever way works for you.

Important note

The information in this book is not intended as a substitute for medical advice. Neither the author nor White Ladder Press can accept any responsibility for any injuries, damages or losses suffered as a result of following the information herein.

A note from the author

You may find it useful to visit my website **www.carolinecarr.com** which contains further information and support, and where you can share your experiences with others.

Chapter 1

How much do you worry?

"Don't worry. Really, you mustn't worry about that. Look, just calm down. You're being ridiculous. Please – stop worrying." Does this seem familiar to you? Perhaps these are the kind of things that people say to you, or that you say to yourself. Maybe you say them to someone else.

Language is a powerful tool, and what a person says can sometimes be unhelpful – even though they don't mean it to be. When you are really worried and anxious, the last thing you need is to feel that you are being ridiculous, or that you are being 'told off'.

The unhelpful messages that we hear often come about through a lack of understanding. Many people do not really understand about worry and anxiety – how it occurs, what it's for, and how severely a person can be affected when they have been too anxious for too long.

You might think:

"I'm worried sick." Well, yes – perhaps you are. You may actually be feeling unwell – especially if you tell yourself that you are worried *sick*. But you know, most of us worry, and in small amounts that's absolutely fine. It's part of the normal, healthy way that we deal with things. When it escalates and gets out of control, that's when worry and anxiety become a real issue. You might be frightened and bewildered by a range of symptoms, and fear that something is medically wrong, or that you are losing your mind.

If you experience alarming physical symptoms and are sometimes overwhelmed with anxiety or panic, you may prefer to go straight to Chapter 4 and read on from there. You can read the rest of this book when you feel ready.

Living with high levels of worry and anxiety can be utterly miserable, but there are loads of things that you can do to help yourself, and that others can do to help you too.

HOW MUCH DO YOU WORRY?

You might be able to identify with some of these:

Rob, 40:
I worry about things sometimes – of course I do. I mean, most people do, don't they? Like when my daughter comes home late and hasn't told us. And if we don't get an order out in time at work. It's that kind of thing. But on the whole, I'm fine. Things don't usually bother me much.

Margaret, 58:
Well I'm usually quite content until I get anxious about something, and then it niggles. Like when our front room needed decorating. It was the ceiling that was getting on my nerves – it looked so shabby, and you see I have arthritis and can't do it myself any more. So there was all the stress of getting someone in to do it, and how much it would cost, and could I trust them. I did get in a bit of a state about that actually.

Bill, 48:
I can't stop worrying. I'm fine a lot of the time and then I just get

worried about things, even when they aren't that important really. I don't know why. I think I've always been like it. I've just learned to live with it.

Isabel, 22:

I feel so nervous sometimes. If I'm asked to give a presentation or anything, I worry about it for weeks before. It's embarrassing really. I think I get more nervous than other people do. I don't think people have any idea how I really feel."

Mike, 28:

I seem to be 'on edge' all the time – just waiting for the next thing to happen. It's hard to explain; it's as if I'm constantly fired up. I dread something happening and not being able to deal with it.

Laura, 21:

It's so scary. Thoughts rushing through my mind, and I feel sick and panicky, and I don't know what to do. I worry in case I might faint.

Joanne, 33:

Sometimes I think I'm going mad. I feel as if I'm watching everything from the outside. It's as if I'm in a different world to everyone else. It's horrible.

People experience worry differently, and in different amounts:

- Small = useful, helping to keep you alert and focused.
- Medium = a nuisance, taking up too much of your time, attention and energy.
- Large = serious. When worry escalates and is out of control, it becomes a terrifying monster which can take over your life.
- Extra large = almost unbearable.

At best, worry is useful and necessary, although the symptoms may be inconvenient. At worst, it can be a living hell.

Worry, anxiety, stress, and nervousness are all terms that describe mental tension and unease. They're often swapped about and used to describe the same things, because they share many similar symptoms.

WORRY

To worry is to be troubled, concerned and bothered by thoughts that disturb you. Everyone worries from time to time, but some people worry and fret more than others.

The word *worry* comes from the old English *wyrgan*, which means 'to strangle'.

ANXIOUS

To be anxious is to be tense, worried and apprehensive.

ANXIETY

If you are in a state of anxiety, you are likely to feel abnormally worried and apprehensive about lots of different things, even when there is no reason to be.

The word *anxious* comes from the Latin *anxius*, which comes from *angere*, meaning 'to choke'.

STRESS

Stress means pressure. When you feel 'stressed' you are under too much mental or emotional strain. You may feel worried and anxious. Although you might be aware that you are under pressure (for example, you might be working too hard) you may not realise how this is affecting you physically and mentally.

The word *stress* appears to be derived from various sources, one of which is from Old French *estresse*, which means 'narrowness, oppression', and from the Latin *strictus*, meaning 'compressed'.

NERVES

Your nerves are part of a highly complex system which forms a network of pathways for carrying signals and impulses between your brain, spinal cord and all the parts of your body. Therefore they are vital to your physical and mental state.

NERVOUSNESS

Nervousness is a state of tension due to an emotional reaction to a situation. So of course your nerves play a part in this. You may be over sensitive, easily alarmed and jumpy. You might feel abnormally uneasy, worried, apprehensive and anxious.

Therefore if someone is said to suffer from 'nerves', or from 'an attack of the nerves', it means that they are experiencing the symptoms of nervousness.

A NERVOUS BREAKDOWN

A nervous breakdown is a breakdown in your mental health; that is, when you are in a state where you are unable to cope with everyday life.

So *worry*, *stress* and *anxiety* have similar meanings, all of which indicate a sense of tightening and constraint. This is exactly what begins to happen to your mind and body as a result of being worried, anxious or stressed.

It is amazing how a few little thoughts can start a whole chain of reactions within your body. Worry is a mental thing – the niggling thoughts, and the churning of things over in your mind.

Thoughts like:

"What if so and so happens? I hope it's going to be all right. If it goes wrong, then what will I do?" And so on. The more you worry, the more it takes hold. And the firmer its grip, the more havoc it can cause. You may experience a whole range of negative emotions too, such as fear, guilt, irritation, anger and sadness, to name but a few.

When you are worried and anxious you become limited and restricted by your own thoughts and feelings. For example, you can spend a large amount of time worrying about something that may never happen, when you could be thinking about or doing something else.

And then there's the physical side of it. Mental worry promotes the stress response – that is, a physical reaction to what you perceive is a threat. Basically, as your body gets ready to deal with this threat, some physical changes take place so that you are ready to deal with whatever it is most effectively. This is explained more in Chapter 7.

When you are worried and anxious, this physical reaction starts and it is quite likely that one of your bodily systems is the one where this is expressed most. For example you may find that:

- Your digestive system is the most affected. You may feel nauseous or be sick as your digestive organs and bowels tighten and squeeze and you may need to go to the toilet.
- Your breathing is affected so that it becomes more shallow or you actually hold your breath.
- You tighten your muscles, so that you tense up.
- You get headaches – due to a 'squeezing' and tightening of the blood vessels in your head.

It is quite possible that your tendency to experience physical symptoms in a particular part of your body is part of a pattern handed down from your family. This might be genetic or it might be learned. For example, perhaps your mother got bad headaches when she was really worried and tense. Maybe you do too.

So how do you personally experience worry and anxiety? The next chapter will help you to explore this and to take steps to prevent it escalating and becoming out of control.

Chapter 2

What do you worry about?

Worry is not a 'thing' that attacks you, or that happens *to* you. You worry because of the way that you think about something. People think about and respond to things differently. What bothers one person won't concern another person at all.

SO WHAT DO YOU WORRY ABOUT?

Do you worry about:

- Something which may or may not happen?
- An event?
- Situation?
- A person?
- Having to make a decision, and whether or not you will make the right one?

Be aware of what triggers worry, stress and anxiety for you. Then if you worry too much, and you want to do something about it, you can.

> **Kerry, 27:**
> I worry about the car. I know it's ridiculous but it's a new car and it was expensive. I mean, it's a great car and I love it, but I'm always worried that something will happen to it. For example, I might bump it or scrape it. And I worry about being able to park it if the space

is too small, especially in multi-storey car parks. I get worried that someone else might damage it. I know it's stupid, because at the end of the day it's only a car, but I can't help it.

Tim, 35:

Money. It's always about money. I mean, no one ever has enough do they? We manage, and my wife works too, but I worry what will happen if I lose my job and we can't pay the mortgage and the bills. I just think: "What will become of us?" I worry about losing our stability, and you know, that will affect the kids' future. Sometimes, if I've had a bad day at work I worry far more. I usually go to the pub to forget about it for a while.

Sandra, 40:

Oh I worry about lots of different things. I always have. One of the things that bothers me is having to entertain and play 'host' to other people. I love to see everyone, but if it's my turn to have everyone round for a meal, I get so worked up about it. I spend days planning and thinking about it, and I know it's unnecessary because they would probably be happy with a ready meal or a takeaway. And the garden. I hate it when the grass isn't cut and it looks untidy. I spend more time worrying about it, and about having to do it, than actually doing it. I know it's silly, but it's just the way I am.

If you want to worry less, you can help yourself by noticing exactly *what* you think, and *when* you think it.

'WHAT IF ...' THOUGHTS

When you are worried about something or somebody, you fear what may or may not happen. These thoughts can niggle, grow and develop. You worry what the outcome *could* be, and what *might* happen. You tend to constantly ask yourself:

"What if (something happens)?" So really, you're living in fear of the future. Like Kerry, Tim and Sandra above.

Kerry would ask herself:
What if something happens to my car? What if I am unable to park it?

Tim would ask himself:
What if I lose my job and we can't pay the mortgage and the bills?

And Sandra – what *exactly* would Sandra ask herself? Is it that she is worried about the cooking, or about seeing her friends, or about having people in her house? Is it that she is worried what people might think if her garden looks untidy? What are the real issues for her? Apart from asking herself questions like:

What if I make a mess of the meal? What if they don't like it? What if they think I'm a bad host? I wonder what her underlying anxieties are. Perhaps, she is also asking herself:
What if I can't cope? What if I let everyone down? What if I let myself down?

Sometimes you have to look below the surface at what it is that really worries you and why.

How you can help yourself to deal with 'What if ...' thoughts

The thoughts and feelings associated with worry are mainly negative and sometimes irrational. If this type of thinking carries on for too long it can become out of control. One of the ways to stop your thoughts from becoming out of control is to challenge them. Do this by asking yourself some more questions. These need to be sensible and down-to-earth, such as:

- How likely is this to happen?
- If it is true, what is the worst that could happen, and how could I deal with this?
- How have I dealt with something similar in the past?
- What would I tell someone else if they were worried and thinking 'what if'?

One of my favourite challenges is very straightforward. Just keep asking yourself:

- And then what would happen?

How you can help someone else to deal with their 'What if ...' thoughts

Ask them questions like the ones above, to help them to challenge their own thinking. And gently encourage them to think in a sensible, rational and down-to-earth way. Add in some positive things too, because when someone worries too much they tend to see the negative side of things too quickly. For example:

Mary has bought a snazzy new dress to wear at a party but as she gets ready to go out she begins to have doubts. She becomes quiet and keeps thinking the same thoughts over and over again:

What if no one else has dressed up? What if I'm overdressed? What if they're all wearing jeans?

Her sister Jo starts to reassure her:

Mary: What if no one else has dressed up?
What if I'm overdressed?
What if they're all wearing jeans?

Jo: So what? Why should it make any difference?
What's the worst that could happen?

Mary: Everyone will think I'm stupid and laugh at me.

Jo: Everyone?

Mary: Well, probably not everyone, but some might.

Jo: But how likely is that to happen? These people are your friends.
And anyway why would it matter?

Mary: Because it'd make me feel terrible and I'd want to leave.

Jo: But why? You look great in that dress! What would be the point of leaving?

Mary: Well, I would feel better.

Jo: Would you? What else would you feel?

Mary: Fed up because I'd be missing out.

Jo: And then what would happen?

Mary: I'd be on my own.

Jo: And then what?

Mary: I'd be miserable.

Jo: Of course you would. Look, what would you tell someone else if they were worrying like this?

Mary: I'd probably tell them there's no point in worrying – just go to the party anyway.

Jo: Mmmm.

Mary: And enjoy it.

Jo: So … ?

Mary: OK – so I'll go!

Convinced, Mary goes to the party and has a great time.

SELF TALK – WHAT DO YOU TELL YOUSELF?

Thoughts are what you say to yourself silently, in your head. So if you tell yourself that you are worried and anxious – you will be. You may also feel powerless to do anything about it. This is because you give yourself that message through the words that you use.

How you can change your self talk

Well, there is no need to feel powerless, because you can change or rearrange the words you use so that the meaning is different. This means that you will see things from a different perspective and feel more in control. This following exercise can take a little time to get used to, but with practice it is worth its weight in gold:

- When you are worried and anxious, just notice your own self talk. Notice *exactly* what words you use when you think. It may help you to write your thoughts down. Just make a note of them as they pop into your head, and make sure that most of them begin with 'I', or have 'I' in them somewhere.

Using 'I' is important, because then you take ownership. Otherwise you may be tempted to write down single words or phrases, such as "Worried," instead of "*I* feel worried," or "Should be able to do this …" instead of "*I* should be able to do this". If you use "I" where it applies to you, then you own the thought or statement, and if you own it, you can change it. I am aware that the term 'I' may not be applicable to every statement, so just experiment and see what happens.

It is likely that your worried thoughts will contain some of the words in bold below:

Can't	I can't stop worrying
Should	I should sort this out
Must	I must get this right
I know	I know they think I'm behaving differently
But	I want to, but I know I won't be able to
If only	If only I could do something to help
Try	I'll try, but it might not make any difference
Difficult	It's really difficult
Problem	That's the problem

- Now think about how you can change and rearrange the words, so that the meaning shifts to enable you to take back control. Like this:

Original word		could become	Preferred word	
Can't 'Can't' really means 'I am unable, I have no control, I am powerless'	I can't stop worrying	→	**Won't** or **Choose**	I won't stop worrying or I choose to worry about this
Should	I should sort this out	→	**Could** or **Decide**	I could sort this out (if I want to and if it will be useful to do so) I choose to sort this out On the other hand, I may decide to do nothing
Must	I must get there on time	→	**Choose**	I choose to get there on time
Know	I know they think I'm behaving differently	→	**Imagine**	I imagine they think I'm behaving differently
But	I want to, but I can't	→	**And**	I want to, and yet I won't right now or I want to, and yet I choose not to
If only	If only I could do something to help	→	**Want**	I want to do something to help
Try	I'll try	→	**Intend**	I intend to do this
Difficult	It's difficult	→	**Tricky**	It's a little tricky

Problem	This is the problem	→	**Opportunity** or **put it in the past tense**	This is an opportunity or This **has been** a problem and now it's an opportunity

Change or rearrange a few words and you can take back control.

How you can help someone change their self talk

- Listen to the words they use and help them to reframe what they say into something more positive.
- If they say that they "*can't*" do something – ask them what they might need to let go of in order to be able to do whatever it is.

THE MESSAGES THAT OTHERS GIVE YOU

What other people say to you is important too. A few words can make all the difference depending on who says them and how you hear them at the time. So if you are feeling particularly sensitive and emotionally wobbly, you can instantly feel battered by someone's comment and it can add to your worry needlessly. So just be aware of this. Now, in your own mind, you can reframe the words they've used, so that their remarks have a more positive effect.

Top worry/anxiety-inducing words that other people might say to or about you are:
(you) should …
(you) must …
if only (you) …
the matter
the problem
like you

There are many others, and you might be aware of certain words that 'get you' every time. Just notice, and quietly change them in your mind.

You may have no control over what a person says to you but you can choose how to think and feel about it.

Chapter 3

What is worry for?

Worry can help you to focus. If there is a situation or an event that you have to face, then it is useful and entirely appropriate to worry as it gets you ready to deal with it to the best of your ability.

George said that during his training to be a doctor, one of the most testing aspects for him was the OSCEs (Objective Structured Clinical Examinations), where medical students' clinical and communication skills are tested. During the OSCEs each student has to visit a number of 'stations' set up with a patient who may be real or an actor, plus an examiner. They are allotted approximately five minutes to demonstrate what they have learned. This involves not only assessing a patient and making a diagnosis but also communicating successfully with them.

George, 30:
I used to get so wound up before the OSCEs. There comes a time when you have so much information in your head that you almost forget that the patient is a real person. I know that sounds awful, but for many of us that's the case. Once you are comfortable with your knowledge base, you can focus on your people skills. Some people are brilliant in dealing with people from the start, but I wasn't because I was always quite shy as I grew up.

So I worried about the OSCEs terribly because I thought I might not

> make it – getting the medical assessment right and dealing with the patient, all in a small room with an examiner sitting there judging everything I did. OSCEs are hair-raising – there are bells to tell you to stop and whistles to tell you to move on to the next person. I hated it every time. But, even so, I did really well and got high marks. I'm sure that even though I got into a state beforehand – feeling sick, light-headed, diarrhoea, clammy hands, dry mouth and so on, once I was in the main room and I was sitting there in front of the first patient, that fear subsided and I was able to concentrate. By the end I was beginning to enjoy it!

So worrying about the situation in George's case was, though unpleasant for him, useful. His fear and apprehension actually helped him to focus and he did well in a situation that he knew he had to deal with, and that he knew would be over in a finite amount of time. There is a difference between being worried and anxious because of an impending situation that is likely to be over soon (such as taking an exam or a driving test), and being worried and anxious about something that may not happen.

It's also important to be aware of *how much* you worry about these events, and for *how long.* If you are over-anxious and fretful for quite some time before the event, and if this is impacting on your life too much, then it is worth taking steps to manage this as effectively as you can.

It would be a good idea to do something about your worrying if:

- you know that you worry about things unnecessarily
- you feel that you just can't stop
- your worrying bothers you and stops you from getting on with your life

Start by considering this:

HOW CAN WORRYING CHANGE OR HELP THE SITUATION?

What can you actually *do* about the situation? Can you personally do something to change the situation that you are worried about? Yes or no?

If the answer is 'yes' then you will need to decide whether or not to do something about it. If the answer is 'no', then that's that. But the question remains: how can the situation be changed or helped by your *worrying* about it? It can't.

You may not be able to do anything to change a situation, but you can choose how to deal with the way that you think and feel about it.

Compassion versus worry

It is heartbreaking to see someone you love suffer, and there are many situations where worry and anxiety, care and compassion become muddled and all blur into one.

Jean, 71

Jean said that she felt "pretty low" sometimes as she looked after her elderly and frail husband. They had been married for almost 50 years and she had watched him decline over the past 18 months. Jean worried constantly about his health.

"I wake in the night and listen to him breathing, and worry that one night I'll wake up and he won't be breathing at all. I worry that I could have done more to help him, and I worry that if he goes soon I won't know how to sort everything out. It's hard when someone is so ill."

Jean said that she felt guilty if she was not worrying. She felt that this was the best she could hope to do – to spend all her time think-

> ing about him, holding him in her thoughts. But she knew she could not change the situation.
>
> She was worried sick (literally), and was fast becoming like a limp, worn-out rag with nothing left to give. Her own inner resources were depleted because she was exhausted and eaten up by the constant worry of it all. Worry, anxiety, stress and compassion had all fused together in her mind.
>
> Eventually, with help and support, Jean accepted the situation for what it was and acknowledged that she was doing all she could for her husband. She began to allow herself to have a life outside of her husband's illness. She started to write her life story "for the grandchildren," and said she found this was really therapeutic. She also took part in an exercise class once a week, and a neighbour was happy to stay with her husband for this short time. Jean developed a new purpose to her life and this helped her to cope.

I am not for one moment suggesting that you should ever act without compassion and tenderness, but there is little point in you sharing another's suffering. If you do, you are in danger of becoming so dragged down and exhausted that you have nothing left to give. You need to think of yourself as a separate package. Look after yourself in order to best help them. Ask yourself if your worrying will actually change or help the situation. The answer is sure to be "No".

WHAT PURPOSE DOES UNNECESSARY WORRY SERVE?

None at all. Unless you benefit from worrying in some way. This is a serious point, because you might actually get something out of worrying and fretting. So ask yourself the following questions. Answer each one in turn:

1. What does worrying give me?
2. What does worrying not give me?
3. If I didn't worry what would that give me?

4 If I didn't worry what would I lose?
5 And then what would happen?

You may be surprised by your answers.

Ellen, 60:
Ellen worried about her son. He left home to marry at the age of 30, and ever since he had gone, she worried about him. Was he happy? Was he eating properly? If he did not contact her for a few days she worried in case he was ill. She liked his wife, and was happy for them both, but still she worried.

When asked these five questions, Ellen thought very seriously before she answered each one:

1 What does worrying give me?
Pain and distress. I don't sleep well sometimes. I wonder how he is. I know it's ridiculous because he's a grown man.

2 What does worrying not give me?
Peace of mind. I should be able to let go.

3 If I didn't worry, what would that give me?
Peace of mind. I'd have to think about other things.

4 If I didn't worry, what would I lose?
I suppose I'd have nothing to focus on in the same way.

5 And then what would happen?
I'd have to find something else to do.

Ellen was surprised to find that her worrying actually filled a gap in her life. It gave her a sense of purpose.

It might be that you're quite comfortable with worrying. Perhaps you think of it as a part of your identity. If this is so – well, you may not want to let it go, like Dave:

> **Dave, 58:**
> I suppose I've always worried since I was a teenager. My mum said I used to worry about everything, especially my health. I used to make her take me to the doctor if I had a sore knee or anything. I'd get myself into such a state. I think I must have been doing it for the attention really. Anyway, it's followed me into later life, because everyone knows I'm a worrier. They joke: "Don't tell Dave about it, 'cos he'll find something to worry about!" I've got a nickname: 'Old Fretface' my mates call me, because I'm always fretting. I don't mind at all – we're all good friends and, well – it's who I am.

If worrying serves some purpose for you, ask yourself if you really want to let go of it. And if you really want to do something about your tendency to worry – you can. Here are a few things that you could do instead:

Think positive thoughts. (For an explanation of why this is important see Chapter 11.)

- Look for the humour in a situation, and laugh a lot
- Sing – even if you think you can't
- Exercise
- Enjoy a new, fun activity
- Phone a cheerful friend for a chat.
- Give yourself a treat for each time you make a firm decision not to worry, and stick to it for a whole day.

LETTING IT GO

We know that a certain amount of appropriate worry is normal and healthy, but too much is not. It can take a while to recognise when you are worrying needlessly. So learning how to observe yourself and to take notice of how and what you think takes practice. Once you have increased your awareness, you can challenge and change each worried thought, as it occurs.

The next step is to learn to let each unhelpful thought go, and to put a positive one in its place. This is much more challenging though, as letting go of a thought *effectively* takes some practice. It's rather like dealing with a toddler who you notice playing with a dangerous toy. If you take the toy away, the child will scream, and then possibly find something equally dangerous to replace it. But if you *immediately* give it a toy which is safe – the child will be content to focus on that instead.

So as soon as you notice that you are thinking something which is unhelpful, tell yourself:

I am letting go of this thought right now. Or
I do NOT need this.

Then immediately replace it with a short positive thought that is meaningful for you. For example:

Everything is working perfectly
Everything is unfolding just as it should
I am doing the best that I can, and brilliantly!
Everything is sorting itself out

So collect a few positive statements that you can use whenever you want to. Then learn them, so that they become quick and easy to repeat.

Chapter 4

Anxiety disorders

Worry and anxiety can escalate and become out of control, but you may not realise that this is what has happened. The first clue that something is wrong could be that you notice alarming physical symptoms.

Andrew, 26:

I kept feeling really sick when I got up in the mornings, and then at random times in the day. I couldn't think what it could be. Then I'd be OK and then a few days later feel really, really sick again for no reason.

Jeni, 28:

I felt like I was going to faint. My heart beat so fast. It would all subside after a few minutes, and I'd be all right. But it kept happening and I didn't know what was the matter with me.

Bill, 31:

I woke up every morning with a really tense jaw. Sometimes I could hardly open my mouth at first, and I was really terrified, I can tell you. After a while it was OK, after a few minutes really. But I was so worried. Anyway, I went to the doctor, and he couldn't find anything wrong and said it was probably tension. I did feel a lot better, knowing there was nothing really wrong with my jaw. My wife said I ground my teeth in my sleep a lot too. It's all better now, but it was frightening while it lasted.

Julie, 23:

I had so much energy after about ten o'clock at night. I used to go out for long walks, which was probably a bit dangerous really, but I just had to use up all this energy. I hardly remember the walks now though – I suppose I was thinking all the time. But I do remember waking up at about 5am some mornings feeling dreadful. It was like this gut-wrenching, terrible apprehension about absolutely everything, and this indescribable loneliness. And then I couldn't get back to sleep. So I'd be exhausted around lunchtime and wide awake late at night. It seemed like a never-ending cycle.

Apart from a range of physical symptoms, you may find that you worry about all sorts of things and feel anxious most of the time, even though there is no obvious reason for doing so. All this can stop you from getting on with your life, and it can be absolute hell. I know this because I went through the experience about 30 years ago, when I was in my early 20s.

Caroline Carr:

It lasted for about two years. I felt absolutely terrible most of the time, but because I had no idea what was the matter with me, and, because I was frightened and confused, I did not seek help for ages.

Quite unexpectedly, I found that I couldn't stand the heat – in fact as soon as it was remotely warm and sunny, I panicked. Other people enjoyed the weather, but to me it was torture. All I could think was: "I've got to get away. I can't stand this." My head would be swimming and I thought I might be sick. Then I'd worry that I might faint, and I'd think: "I've fainted before, so it's bound to happen again. I'm sure it's going to happen now – any moment." My thoughts would race – I'd be thinking the same thing over and over. And I'd be intensely aware of my heart beating.

"It's beating too fast. I need to go to the lavatory. I'm going to faint. I was sick the other day – I feel sick again. There must be something

> medically wrong." Then I'd remember that breathing deeply was supposed to help, so I'd try really hard and focus on breathing out slowly. But almost immediately the irrational thoughts would take over again, and I'd tell my self that it wasn't working and I just had to get away. As time went on, I couldn't stand the cold either; or to be in crowds, in a pub, a restaurant, a cinema or theatre, on a bus, a train, in a waiting room, or in a queue. But I had absolutely no idea why. That's what scared me.
>
> I felt so lonely – yet I was in a loving, steady relationship. The whole episode was undeniably awful at the time, and it was miserable and perplexing for my partner too. I thought that I was 'odd'. One of the few places where I really felt at ease was in my own flat – safely cocooned in my own environment. And asleep. I loved to sleep. I remember thinking sometimes: "This is what it must be like to be a tired, middle-aged person, who doesn't want to go out anywhere, or do anything."

When I finally did go to the doctor, I got the impression that he wasn't sure what was the matter with me. In fact, I reckon he was completely baffled. Now, this would be recognized as a mental health issue and taken very seriously. Now, I believe that what I experienced then may have been an anxiety disorder of some sort.

When anxiety becomes extreme or irrational, causes you distress and interferes with your life, it ceases to be normal, healthy anxiety. It becomes an anxiety disorder.

ANXIETY DISORDERS

Anxiety disorders are divided into various categories, and each category has its own symptoms. To be honest, when you're feeling absolutely terrible you probably don't really care what category your symptoms are under. You are overwhelmed and bewildered and you just want to feel normal again. All you want is for it to stop. Well, the good news is that it will – eventually. But be prepared for this to take some time.

Below is a list of symptoms that you might potentially experience if you have an anxiety disorder of some kind. Of course, you could experience any of these anyway, whether you have an anxiety disorder or not. The point is that if they are affecting your life, and you are unable to get on with your normal day-to-day activities, then there could be cause for concern.

Usually symptoms are separated out according to which category of anxiety disorder they relate to. But they are all listed together here because you could experience any of them, and what you really need to know is that other people have experienced them too. So take strength from the fact that you are not alone in how you feel – millions of others go through this too.

The following symptoms do not all appear on the standard medical lists but every single one of them has been contributed by someone who has lived through an anxiety disorder.

- Intense, frequent and seemingly uncontrollable worry and anxiety about all sorts of things
- Feeling frightened although you may not know why
- Feeling unable to cope in certain situations, and so avoiding them
- Racing thoughts
- A sensation that everything's coming together and all at once
- Nausea
- Fainting
- Feeling as if you could faint but not doing so
- Diarrhoea
- Constipation
- Stomach pains
- Craving food at random times

- Trouble getting to sleep
- Waking up at odd times
- Nightmares or 'weird' dreams
- Sudden bursts of energy when you least expect them, for example late at night.
- Headaches
- Feeling breathless
- Holding your breath
- Feeling that your heart is beating too quickly or too slowly
- Pains in your joints
- Tightness in your muscles
- Shaking
- Chest pains and tightness
- Sweating
- Tense jaw – feeling you can't open your mouth
- Very dry mouth
- Feeling exhausted
- Restlessness
- Inability to concentrate
- Can't remember things
- Irritability
- Feel as if you are 'going mad'
- Feel as if you are detached from everyone and the world around you
- Feel as if you are watching yourself from 'outside'
- Feeling paranoid that people are looking at you or talking about you
- A feeling that you're being watched
- Unable to relax
- Fidgety
- Dizziness
- Increased sensitivity to noise
- Feeling very cold

- Feeling suddenly very hot
- Wanting to escape, or get away from a place/situation
- Twitching
- Legs feel like jelly
- Numbness or tingling sensations
- Vertigo
- Sight and/or hearing affected
- Crying spells
- Lack of appetite
- Really low moods
- A sense of much time having passed, when in fact it's only a few minutes
- Underlying sense of apprehension
- Pins and needles
- Difficulty in swallowing
- Frightened that you might lose control
- Can't switch off
- Feel that you are being obsessive about some things
- Fear of dying
- Over-sensitive to the weather – the temperatures, air pressure, bright sunlight, grey 'muggy' days
- Over-concern about health issues. For example, if you have a headache, you may be certain that it is a brain tumor
- Periods of feeling incredibly lonely and isolated
- Over-sensitive to different places and situations

You may experience several of these symptoms over a period of time, plus other seemingly unconnected ones. For example, it is not unusual to discover changes to your skin, such as rashes and spots and eczema-type irritations; and if you are female, there may be changes in your menstrual cycle.

DO YOU NEED TO GO TO THE DOCTOR?

Yes, because you need to know that your symptoms are not being caused by something else. So if you have been living with some of these symptoms for a few weeks, if they are stopping you from getting on with your day-to-day life, and if you feel overwhelmed and frightened, you definitely need to see your GP. You might be reluctant to do this for a variety of reasons, some of which are:

- Concern that the doctor will think that you are being ridiculous
- You are worried that you might actually be very ill
- You do not want to take any medication offered

Yet it is really important to go to the doctor if the way that you feel affects you so much that it prevents you from getting on with your life. Your symptoms could be caused by something such as another illness, or as a result of medication you are taking, and the only way to be sure about this is to seek medical advice. A doctor can do various tests in order to eliminate any other possible causes.

Assuming that there is no underlying medical reason, the doctor will ask you a range of questions and check your symptoms in order to make a diagnosis. You may leave the surgery feeling reassured, valued and helped. On the other hand, you might be worried that you haven't been listened to properly, and that you are a hopeless case. Be aware that:

- Your doctor may need to see you more than once before being able to make a firm diagnosis. This is because doctors have guidelines which help to provide a diagnostic tool. If in the course of seeing a person and hearing what they have to say, they decide that they do not meet these, then they may see no need for further action at that point. *It may be that by returning after a week or two the patient does meet these criteria, and the response may be quite different.*

- When you go to the doctor, it can be helpful to take someone else with you. They may remember symptoms and behaviours that you have forgotten – and it is very easy to forget exactly how you felt after the moment has passed. Also, another person's concern is unlikely to go unnoticed.
- Doctors are incredibly busy people, and they have a vast amount of knowledge. As with all of us, they are individuals, each with their own style and way of doing things. And, as with all of us, some are better at interpersonal communication skills than others. If you feel dissatisfied and unhappy with your treatment, make an appointment to see someone else at a later date. This could make all the difference.
- Your doctor may refer you to:
  - a therapist or nurse at the surgery
  - a psychiatrist – that is, a medical doctor who specialises in diagnosing and treating mental illness
  - a clinical psychologist – that is, a mental health professional who can assess mental and emotional disorders and provide therapy for these.

The armed forces are experts in dealing with the effects of high levels of anxiety and stress. Group Captain Geoff Reid, Defence Consultant Advisor in Psychiatry for the Armed Forces, makes the following point, which is good advice for everyone:

"It's important to understand that to feel bad doesn't necessarily mean that you're ill. Sometimes things do hurt, and it hurts because we're human. It doesn't mean that you're psychiatrically ill or that you have anything wrong with you, and it's generally going to get better if you do good, sensible things, like get support and rest. But there is a need to recognise that sometimes it's more than that, and if it's extreme or goes on too long, or is inappropriate in some way, then people should go and seek advice."

Chapter 5

Categories of anxiety disorders

Anxiety disorders are complex and so they can be tricky to diagnose. It's not like dealing with a broken leg, where the symptoms are fairly obvious and the treatment is therefore reasonably straightforward. Like knotted balls of wool, these disorders need to be disentangled so that they can be dealt with properly.

For a start, there is a range of mental, emotional, physical and behavioural symptoms to consider. Also, the way individuals experience worry, anxiety, stress and fear differs. So in order to help with this process, mental health professionals have divided anxiety disorders into several main categories, and each of these has its own symptoms and characteristics. This helps a doctor to make a diagnosis and select the most suitable treatment. Often more than one of the disorders exists together, so each needs to be separately recognised and treated in its own right. The most common categories are:

- **Generalized Anxiety Disorder** (**GAD**) is persistent and excessive worry and anxiety over a range of different things. There might not seem to be any specific reason for this, but you feel as if you are on edge all the time. This is probably the most common form of anxiety disorder.
- **Panic Attacks** – you may feel fine one moment and then – wham! It hits you, a sudden overwhelming sense of anxiety and fear, cou-

pled with intense physical symptoms. This is so scary that you might think that you are having a heart attack or a stroke, and fear that you won't be able to cope. You worry so much that it will happen again that you live in fear of your own fear. Panic attacks often occur with another anxiety disorder, and although they are terrifying they are not dangerous.

- **Agoraphobia** – this is where you fear places and situations: in case you can't escape, in case there might be no one to help you if you have a panic attack, and in case you embarrass yourself in public. Such places include crowds, public places and public transport. Therefore you may restrict yourself to staying where you feel safe.

- **Specific Phobias** are when you have an inappropriately intense fear of something or somewhere. Contact with, or the thought of coming into contact with, your feared object, place or situation can lead to symptoms of panic. You become desperate to avoid whatever you have a phobia of, and this in turn can lead to panic or anxiety attacks.

- **Social Anxiety Disorder (Social Phobia)** is a fear of specific social situations where you are worried what other people might think of you, such as speaking in public. The symptoms of social phobias are very similar to those of other phobias, and also include blushing, trembling or an urgent need to go to the toilet.

- **Post Traumatic Stress Disorder** (**PTSD**) is an intense recurring anxiety, fear, flashbacks and horror, having experienced or witnessed an unusually traumatic event. In the First World War it was called 'shell shock', after the memories of soldiers who had been in the trenches. Now it is understood that any traumatic situation can cause PTSD, for example, personal abuse and rape, serious accidents, natural disasters, terrorist attacks, military combat and any situation where a person has felt intense horror and helplessness. This is much more serious than merely becoming 'upset' by remembering something unpleasant. Though the effects can in some cases last for years, the majority of people recover and, with good treatment and help, the symptoms go away.

- **Obsessive Compulsive Disorder** (**OCD**) is characterised by obsessive thoughts that cause you anxiety. In order to relieve this you may perform rituals or repetitive actions.

  Obsessions are images, thoughts or urges that keep coming into your mind, and often include worrying excessively about something, like the fear that you might have hurt someone, worrying about illness, death and germs, or having intrusive sexual thoughts or urges.

  Compulsions are the thoughts or actions that you then feel compelled to do or repeat, such as excessive checking, hand washing, cleaning, touching, arranging, hoarding, counting and measuring.

There can also be physical symptoms with OCD, and these are very similar to those of a panic attack.

You may want to research anxiety disorders further, and there is a mass of information available in books and on the internet. But be aware that you could easily become confused. Within these categories there are often sub-categories, and more names and labels to consider – and potentially this could make you worry more.

Depression – the 'Black Dog'

There are similarities between depressive illness and anxiety disorders, but they are not the same thing.

They often occur together though, and it is worth being mindful of the following:

- People who are depressed are often highly anxious.

- People who are overwhelmed with anxiety can behave in a way that is similar to someone who is depressed.
- Occasionally, an anxiety disorder such as GAD can be misdiagnosed as depression.
- The age of a person when they first experience symptoms could affect the diagnosis. "*There is an old rule of thumb in psychiatry that anybody presenting with anxiety symptoms over the age of 35 or 40 onwards for the first time, in the absence of an exceptional stressor, has depressive illness until proved otherwise. The anxiety symptoms could be a manifestation of something else.*" Group Captain Geoff Reid, Defence Consultant Advisor in Psychiatry for the Armed Forces.

The Depression Alliance lists the most common symptoms of general depression as:

- Tiredness and loss of energy
- Persistent sadness
- Loss of self-confidence and self-esteem
- Difficulty concentrating
- Not being able to enjoy things that are usually pleasurable or interesting
- Undue feelings of guilt or worthlessness
- Feelings of helplessness and hopelessness
- Sleeping problems – difficulties in getting off to sleep or waking up much earlier than usual
- Avoiding other people, sometimes even your close friends
- Finding it hard to function at work/college/school

- Loss of appetite
- Loss of sex drive and/or sexual problems
- Physical aches and pains
- Thinking about suicide and death
- Self-harm

Depression Alliance 020 7633 0557 www.depressionalliance.org

A milder form of depression becomes a serious depression when someone's life is severely affected. The sort of things that can happen are:

- The person is likely to cut down their activites.
- Things that they have enjoyed doing in the past, and friends whose company they have valued, may begin to matter less.
- They may have no energy, to the extent that they can't be bothered to get out of bed, or even talk.
- There is a general 'shrinking in'. That is, their outlook and horizons shrink in until there is a black hopeless and helpless core in the middle.
- It may be that the person who is depressed ceases to have an external awareness or concern about themselves. For example, they may hold a belief such as this: "Nothing can help me. I'll never be happy again. Things are only getting worse. My own body doesn't matter so why should I bother to wash it, or feed it, or clothe it?"
- They may feel that there is no point in anything and that there is no way out of their own hopelessness and helplessness.
- They may have thoughts of and talk about suicide – especially as they recover and their energy returns.

Like an anxiety disorder, depression can affect anyone at any time in their life. It can creep up slowly or hit suddenly, like a bolt out of the blue. But one of the key differences is that depression is to do with helplessness and hopelessness, and a shrinking inwards. Severe anxiety is about fear of the future, and what might or might not happen, and generally the individual will mentally search for future possible threats to themselves, and worry about the consequences.

As with anxiety disorders, there are various categories and types of depression, so these can add to the complexity of making a diagnosis.

TREATMENT

Within the Western culture, the type of treatments that you are likely to be offered for anxiety disorders and depression are:

- Medication
- Psychotherapy, such as:
  - *Counselling* to help people cope with problems they are experiencing.
  - *CBT (Cognitive Behavoural Therapy)* which looks at the relationship between thoughts and feelings. It helps the person to see things in a different way, and to practise coping skills in situations that they find awkward or traumatic. This can take place on a one-to-one basis, and sometimes in groups. If you are offered a group, go for it. Avoid being put off by your fear that you may be 'worse' than anyone else, or that you may feel so overwhelmed that you need to run out of the room. The other group members will understand. They will be just as fearful as you are, and you will be amazed by the support and help you will get from each other. Group work is very powerful. See it as a great opportunity for you.

For PTSD the following is also often used:

EMDR (Eye Movement Desensitisation and Reprocessing). An EMDR therapist offers a range of ways to help the person process the trauma. For example, the person may be asked to make specific eye movements whilst recalling a traumatic incident. This is only one of the methods used in EMDR and there are many theories about how and why this works. You might like to read more about this on www.emdr.org.uk

Many people find that medication is a great help. Often this is combined with some form of counselling or CBT. Equally, others never take medication at all and find that, for example, a course of CBT is all they need.

Sometimes people go to a counsellor and think:

"At last. Someone who will understand and be able to help me." Occasionally, they leave feeling disappointed because they feel they have been judged, or because the counsellor's manner was not what they'd expected. Be aware that the most highly qualified therapist may not necessarily be the right one for you. Give them a chance, but remember that they too are human, and it might just be that you don't develop a good rapport. Try someone else instead. This can make a huge difference. You have to feel comfortable with your therapist. If you have been referred for therapy by your GP, explain that you would like to see someone else if possible, and be prepared for the fact that this could take time because of the availability of resources. If you decide to find your own therapist, make sure that they belong to a recognised professional register, and be prepared for the fact that you will probably have to pay.

British Association for Counselling and Psychotherapy (BACP)
0870 443 5252 www.bacp.co.uk

United Kingdom Council for Psychotherapy (UKCP). 020 7014 9955
www.psychotherapy.org.uk

Helen, 22

I think I'd been building up to it all my life, all through school and everything. I didn't realise at the time. It was awful. I've never felt so scared or so lonely in my life. I went to the doctor at university, which at first was not a helpful experience because I left feeling that I was just being a nuisance. But I went again after another week and saw someone else. He gave me a load of blood tests and examined me, and really reassured me. He arranged for some counselling, and actually I saw two different people. The first one assessed me, and I just didn't like her – in fact she made me feel worse. When I said I felt odd because I couldn't face doing lots of things, she seemed to agree with me. I felt that she thought I **was** odd. To be honest, I left the room feeling like a freak. But then I was referred for CBT and that was better. The counsellor there gave me exercises to do and explained everything and was far more understanding. That was a huge relief, and it did help. Just knowing that I wasn't crazy helped, and knowing that there were things I could do. It took months and months before I began to feel remotely 'normal' again, but at least I felt I knew how to manage things. I felt I had some control back. I do think it's important to feel in control, and it's so easy to lose that when you're so frightened. I felt I could trust the second counsellor and that she understood. That really helped.

ALTERNATIVE AND COMPLEMENTARY TREATMENTS

There is a range of alternative and complementary treatments that also treats anxiety disorders successfully. However, it is vital that you go to the doctor in the first instance in order to eliminate any other causes for your symptoms. Whatever treatment you choose, it has to be the one you feel most comfortable with. My particular favourites in the treatment of anxiety disorders are: Hypnotherapy, Neuro-

Linguistic Programming (NLP), Homeopathy, Nutrition Therapy and Acupuncture. Not all of these are scientifically proven, but many people feel that they work for them.

- See your GP first to eliminate any other possible causes for your symptoms, and then find out about treatments that appeal to you.
- Check which are the main professional registers for each therapy and make sure the therapist you choose is a member of one.
- Be clear about what the therapist needs from you on your first visit, and prepare this.
- Be completely honest. Tell your therapist what they need to know and answer their questions as best as you can. Avoid withholding information because you think it may not be relevant. Your therapist is there to help, and usually the more information you can give them the better.
- It may help to take someone with you who knows you well. Your perception of how you behave might be quite different from what someone else might notice. Also, you might forget just how intensely you experienced your symptoms at the time. For example, a man with an anxiety disorder went to see a Homeopath with his wife. Their conversation went like this:

  Homeopath: How are things?

  Man: Fine at the moment …

  Homeopath: And how's your churning stomach now?

  Man: Oh it's OK.

  Man's wife: But just yesterday on the bus – you said twice that your stomach was turning over and that you needed to get off.

  Man: Yes – I'd forgotten that.

Homeopath: How are you sleeping?

Man: Fine.

Man's wife: No you're not. You scream out in your sleep.

Taking someone with you can help a therapist to get a clearer picture sometimes, especially if you have forgotten the details. Then after they have got the information they need, they will usually see you on your own. However, this is entirely up to you, and it may be that you would feel far more comfortable seeing a therapist on your own.

- Once you have embarked on a treatment, stick with it. Medications and remedies can take a while to kick in, and it may well take some time before you notice any difference. If, after a while you do not feel that what you are doing or taking is helpful, tell your therapist. If you have been prescribed treatment by a doctor, or if you have been seeing an alternative or complementary therapist, they need to know if the treatment doesn't seem to be working. It may be that you need something else. Be open and honest with them and give them a chance to help you. They will not think you are stupid for getting in touch. In fact, many therapists will be happy to receive and reply to texts and emails.

Many alternative and complementary therapies have to be paid for privately but therapists usually offer free initial consultations or screening. There are insurance schemes that cover at least some of the cost. And look out for places where you can try treatments cheaply, for example colleges where students are properly supervised, and complementary health fairs where you can talk to therapists and sometimes have taster sessions.

If at any time you just need someone to talk to, or some support, do contact one of the many mental health organisations that are available. Some offer email support and all of them have great websites with masses of information. Most have helplines that you can telephone (although not all of them are available for 24 hours), and I would strongly encourage you to make use of these. Just being able to talk to someone who understands can be a huge relief. For example:

The Samaritans 08457 90 90 90 (24 hour helpline)
www.samaritans.org

SANE 0845 767 8000 www.sane.org.uk

Mind 0845 766 0163 www.mind.org.uk.

Know that there is no shame in telephoning a mental health helpline when you need support. That is exactly what they are for – and they are fantastic.

Gudrun, 33:
When I met Gudrun, she talked constantly for one hour. It was clear that she was highly anxious, but it was also clear that her issues were very complex. She was able to tell me a great deal about her situation, but also that 'Nothing works.' Some of the things that she said were:

"People assume that I can do stuff, but I can't. I can do the high level stuff, but not the simple things, like sort out my flat. I'm sleeping on the floorboards – I can't seem to organise anything. But if someone asks me to do an art workshop for 50 people – I can get that together really well. And going places - sometimes I've no idea how I got there or how to get back. I can walk round for hours and forget where I need to be.

I've got a very sensitive nervous system – I feel things intensely. I have been given medication, but I lied to my GP. I told her I was taking it, but I wasn't. You see, part of my problem is that I sabotage myself – I can't stick with things. I take things on and then I stop. I've had 19 different therapists and every one tells me something different. Everyone's giving up on me now.

I've been told I may be bipolar (manic depressive), and I used to have eating disorders. I still review my food plans and sometimes I binge and then make myself sick. One doctor said I might have ME. I'm also obsessive compulsive about some things – I've been told that. I can't sleep at night because I can't stop thinking. I get scared by my own thoughts. I feel overwhelmed and emotionally crippled – I'm overwhelmed by growing up."

Gudrun looked totally distraught. She also told me that she had been sexually abused when she was 12, and that she had attempted suicide three times in the last five years.

Gudrun's story is included here because it is a good example of how multi-faceted a person's mental condition might be. There were numerous issues to unravel, and over the years she had got into the position where she had become completely overwhelmed with masses of information from various doctors, psychiatrists, psychologists and therapists. She'd also spent hours on the internet, researching her symptoms and various treatments. She mistrusted all medication and so refused to take it. She was constantly searching for the right help and it had got to the point where she perceived that everyone was telling her something different. So all the information was going round and round in her head and adding to any anxiety that she'd had to start with. Gudrun's case was very complex, but if she had trusted a therapy and stuck to it, I feel that her story could have been quite different.

Chapter 6

History – who gets anxiety disorders and why?

HISTORY

Mental disorder and depressive illness is not a new, modern condition. There are references to it throughout history. For example, the Ancient Greeks referred to people who had a fear of leaving their homes as being 'Agoraphobic', which means 'fear of the marketplace'; and legend says that when the Greek god Pan was awoken from his sleep, people became overwhelmed with an irrational fear – hence 'panic'. It is thought that Charles Darwin may have had both panic attacks and agoraphobia, and that Sigmund Freud may have had some sort of anxiety disorder too. Sir Isaac Newton, Robert Burns, Alfred Lord Tennyson, Charlotte Bronte, Emily Dickinson and Abraham Lincoln were all thought to be affected by some form of 'nervous illness'. If you are interested in this, the internet is a great place to find out more. Key 'history of anxiety disorders' into a search engine.

A couple of hundred years ago those who were most severely affected with depressive and 'nervous illnesses' were looked after in hospital, but if their symptoms were mild to moderate they just got on with their lives as best as they could because there was nothing else that could be done. Now we have a much greater understanding.

WHO GETS ANXIETY DISORDERS?

According to NHS Direct in 2007 [www.nhsdirect.nhs.uk]:

- About 1 in 50 people are affected by Generalized Anxiety Disorder at some time in their life.
- 1% to 2% of men and women have a social phobia.
- Approximately 5% of adults develop agoraphobia.
- At least 1 in 10 people have occasional panic attacks.
- 5% of men and 10% of women are affected by PTSD at some time in their life.
- 2% of the population is affected by OCD.

It is generally thought that more women than men are affected but from my own research I would suggest that anxiety disorders affect a great many men too.

Unfortunately, a key time for anxiety disorders and phobias to manifest is during young adulthood, often in the early 20s. This may be because this is a time of great change for many people. It's a shame though, because it can mean that that the affected person misses out on loads of things because they feel so bad. However, OCD can start at a very young age and develop more fully later on. Anxiety disorders can be triggered by an event, but they can also develop slowly and build up over time.

So basically, anyone can develop an anxiety disorder at any time, regardless of age or culture.

WHY DO PEOPLE GET ANXIETY DISORDERS?

Research has shown that some people may be more likely to develop anxiety disorders whilst others do not. This can be due to any of the following reasons, or a combination of several:

Health – it can occur because of an illness or medical condition. For example, you may have had a debilitating illness such as a virus. Research shows that nutrition affects mental health.

Drugs – it can come about as a result of substance abuse. It can also be a side effect of some medications. It is worth realising that overdosing on caffeine and stimulant drinks can also cause symptoms consistent with anxiety disorders.

Genetic – if there is a family history of anxiety disorder, a person *may* be more vulnerable to developing a disorder themselves.

Biological a change can occur in the chemicals in the brain which therefore affects a person's thoughts and feelings.

Psychological – a person may have certain characteristics that could mean they are more likely to develop an anxiety disorder. The way that they think and feel about themselves and the world around them plays a part. So for example, they may have a sense that they have no control over their life, and worry excessively about things. They may be unable to cope adequately with difficult situations or stress.

Environmental – the things that happen in a person's life can contribute to their developing an anxiety disorder.

- General distress. Anxiety can gradually build up, without there appearing to be any major problems in the person's life. However they may find it tricky to cope with everyday things because of the way that they feel.

- The person may find a problem or situation overwhelming, for example they may feel overwhelmed by responsibility. Some people describe not wanting to grow up – perhaps because of something that they feel the may lose, or because of the extra responsibilities that adulthood brings.
- There may have been a trauma, or unduly stressful event, and the person may or may not know what that was or when it occurred. Sometimes the memory of a trauma has lain dormant for years, and then it is triggered by something and the symptoms of an anxiety disorder begin to kick in. For example, it is quite common for the memory of an event which happened in childhood to be filed away in the subconscious, only to resurface in adulthood when something 'gives it a nudge'.

Personality – there is a theory that particular personality traits can affect the way people respond to situations and how they experience and handle stress.

In the 1950s, a famous investigation was conducted by American cardiologists Friedman and Rosenman into which type of person was most likely to have heart disease. They discovered that typically these people were extremely driven, competitive, impatient, energetic and ambitious. They set themselves high standards and almost impossible deadlines and workloads. They referred to this group as 'Type A'. The group who did not have the same sense of urgency and drive seemed to take life more slowly, were more relaxed and less likely to develop heart disease. This group was referred to as 'Type B'. As more research was carried out, further personality types were recognised.

You might find that an understanding of different personality types could be useful to you because you may recognize traits in yourself which explain how you personally are likely to react to various levels of stress, and therefore how vulnerable you are likely to be to its negative effects. Should you want to explore this further, there is plenty of literature available, and the internet is a good place to start.

Anyone can have an anxiety disorder, regardless of where they live. Someone living quietly in the countryside is just as likely to develop an anxiety disorder as someone living in a large city. However, if it's tranquillity that you need, then it is worth bearing the following in mind:

Ten factors that spell tranquillity

according to research by the Campaign to Protect Rural England [www.cpre.org.uk]

In order of importance, the top 10 factors deemed to make a place 'tranquil' are:

1. Seeing natural landscapes
2. Hearing birdsong
3. 'Hearing' peace and quiet
4. Seeing natural woodland
5. Seeing the stars at night
6. Seeing streams
7. Seeing the sea
8. Hearing natural sounds such as leaves rustling, wind blowing
9. Hearing wildlife noises such as sheep bleating and cows mooing
10. Hearing the sound of natural water such as rivers babbling and waves crashing

To sum up, the majority of anxiety disorders occur because something is not 'right' with that person, whatever their predisposition might be. It is the body's way of saying: "Wait a moment, something's not right here, and it needs sorting out."

Chapter 7

How to help yourself immediately

Sam, 28, had experienced several of the symptoms listed on pages 28–30 for about two months:

> I went to the Doctor because I thought I must be really ill. I've been told there's nothing medically wrong and that I have severe anxiety symptoms. I'm going for some counselling next week. Sometimes I feel OK, and then suddenly I think I'm going completely mad. My whole body seems to sieze up. I can't do the sort of things I like doing in case I feel terrible. I'm so scared. I feel like my life is out of control. I'd do anything, and I mean **anything,** to feel better. I just don't know how to deal with this.

How to help yourself immediately

Know that:

- You are not 'mad' or 'crazy'.
- There is also a very good chance that there is absolutely nothing medically wrong with you, even though you might be convinced that there is. But you do need to go to the doctor in order to be clear about this.
- The frightening symptoms that you experience are simply part of a process.

- Thousands of other people are experiencing symptoms too, and they are just as bewildered by them as you are.
- You will feel better. It just may take some time.

So what you need to do is to keep the following words firmly in your mind at all times:

1. **UNDERSTAND – what is happening**
2. **ACCEPT – what is happening**
3. **ALLOW – it to happen**

Honestly, these are the most important words to remember because they encapsulate the process that will help you to feel better.

Read the information under each of these headings and become familiar with it. They may be all you need.

UNDERSTAND what is happening

The Stress Response – a very basic explanation

If you see a hungry lion running purposefully towards you, you are bound to realise that you're in danger. The chances are you will want to get out of the way as fast as you can. On the other hand, you might decide to stay put and fight it off. Either way, your mind will instruct your body to get ready to deal with an immediate emergency. Therefore within seconds, various chemicals are released into your bloodstream and extra energy will rush through your body to prepare you for action. This is known as the 'stress response' or 'fight-or-flight' – specifically designed to enable you to survive. It has evolved within human beings over thousands of years and it kicks in as soon as you experience a danger or a threat.

All sorts of physical changes occur as part of this process.

- Your heart rate increases and your muscles become tense.
- Extra supplies of blood and oxygen are sent to the muscles that need it most, reducing the flow to your skin and to your stomach. (So you may become pale, and feel the need to go to the lavatory.)
- Your digestion slows down or stops.
- Your breathing becomes faster, like an athlete ready for action, but you may also feel tightness in your chest and slightly dizzy or light-headed.
- You may sweat (so that your body does not overheat whilst in action).
- Mentally you focus entirely on the perceived threat.

When the danger (or what you thought was the danger) is over, the body restores itself back to normal. So the 'stress response' is a perfectly natural response to a situation that you see as a threat.

Similarly, when you are really anxious and worried, and when you are under stress, your body responds by getting ready to deal with an emergency. This is just how it is. There may be no crisis to deal with, but because of your high level of anxiety and stress your body gets the message that you need to prepare to deal with some threat immediately. So it does its job and prepares you for action, putting you in a state of high alert. The emergency chemicals flood your system, preparing you to run away quickly or stay and fight. But you might not be in a position to do either.

For example, you might be worried and anxious about something at work. You may feel threatened and vulnerable, but be powerless to do anything about it, as it's out of your control. As you keep returning to the same thoughts and feelings of worry and anxiety, and as the stress builds, chemicals flood through your body to prepare you for action – but you can't use them correctly, because you are not dealing with an emergency. They're still floating around though, and you are still in a state of "Go!"

Unless your body is allowed to release and return to normal, the impact of this builds up. Your body is ready for action, but it simply doesn't act. Everything piles up, so that you are in an ongoing state of tension. This is not good, as this is when it can start to affect your day-to-day life, and then it can escalate and become out of control.

You may want to know more details about the stress response, and about how each of your symptoms occurs and why. Information is easily available about this, but I would avoid getting too involved in the mechanics and too concerned with the finer details. There is the potential to become more confused, and therefore more worried and anxious.

Worry, nervousness, anxiety or stress act as warnings of a possible threat to you. They only become a problem when they are experienced out of context or when they become really exaggerated.

You might be really surprised to learn that a process as natural as the 'stress response' is responsible for your symptoms. All those terrifying thoughts and sensations are simply due to an overworked nervous system, and nothing more sinister. So now that you know this, you can begin to relax, safe in the knowledge that no harm will come to you.

The armed forces are experts in dealing with anxiety disorders:

"The motto of the parachute training school is: 'Knowledge Defeats Fear'. What we do is teach people about these issues before they go on

deployment. They have briefings from the mental health services and others on exactly what to expect. So knowing what the issues might be doesn't encourage the issues, it helps people to deal with them." Group Captain Geoff Reid, Defence Consultant Advisor in Psychiatry for the Armed Forces.

You may never know the *exact* reason why you feel so bad. But you may have been building up worry, anxiety and stress for some time and the range of symptoms that you experience are simply the body's way of saying "Stop! Time to do something about this."

ACCEPT what is happening

So let's just **stop** for a moment, and consider this:

You are **Scared** because you feel **Terrible**. The physical and mental sensations that you experience alarm you, and so you probably believe that something is medically wrong. You are so worried and anxious that you feel that you are **Out of Control**. Your immediate reaction is to fight this, and you put **Pressure** on yourself to find answers and to make the symptoms go.

Well, actually it's not helpful to put up resistance. Fighting anxiety feeds it. When you fight the symptoms, more stress response chemicals are released into your system to prepare you for action. So as these continue to build up, the symptoms are more likely to intensify, not subside.

We know through research that the stress response follows a set pattern. It brings about all these physical and mental changes to keep you safe. It's only doing its job. Once you understand that this is what is happening – accept it. Avoid adding to it by becoming more and more anxious and frightened. There's no point in trying to stop it and get rid of the symptoms, because that won't work. It's happening. And do you know what? It's OK.

The moment you accept what is happening instead of fighting against it, is the moment when you start to win.

A whole new process begins:

1 You accept that there is a reason for your symptoms, and that you are OK, and that no harm will come to you.

2 So you are relieved, because you now know that, although your symptoms may be unpleasant and uncomfortable, this is all that they are. They are no longer terrifying and bewildering, because now you understand how they come about and why they occur, and that they are not dangerous at all.

3 Because you understand what is happening to you, you are no longer frightened. There is no threat and no danger, so there is no need for the stress response to kick in. Those emergency chemicals aren't needed any more because you aren't giving them any reason to exist.

However, what the mind and body accepts, takes time. If you have experienced symptoms of an anxiety disorder for some time, it may take a while before you notice any positive changes.

ALLOW it to happen

Once, when I went to the fair, I had a ride on the waltzers. It all started well and then suddenly, things changed. Everything speeded up. The music got louder. The waltzer cars began to go round and round and up and down all at once. We twisted and stopped for a second, and twisted the other way. We were thrown to one side of the car – and then to the other. It went on and on, twisting and turning, and round and round and up and down. There was no respite. I felt sick, and hot and sweaty, and I thought I would faint. All I wanted was for it to stop, but it seemed to go on for ever. The music was driving me crazy. I hated it. But what could I do? Absolutely nothing. So I just hung on in there and put up with it, knowing that it would end eventually and I'd be all right again. After a few minutes the ride stopped. I felt as if I had been to hell and back. I climbed out and wobbled down the steps. I wanted to creep into a hole and be sick.

Well, I was not sick. In fact, I was fine. Admittedly it took a while before the feelings subsided, but I managed to enjoy the rest of the fair. Whilst I was in that waltzer car I knew that although I felt dreadful, I had to let the whole thing take its course. I knew the ride would come to an end eventually, and that I would be all right again.

Eventually your symptoms will find their own level and sort themselves out. Just allow them to be, and they will pass in the fullness of time.

HOW LONG DOES AN ANXIETY DISORDER LAST?

This is like asking "how long is a piece of string?" It's impossible to say because everyone is different, and the whole area of anxiety disorder is complex.

You might just wake up one day and be aware that you are absolutely fine. This does happen sometimes. But it is more likely to be a gradual process. In fact, many people are reluctant to say that they are 'better', but they might say that they are 'cautiously optimistic'. Usually you know you are getting there when you realise that you no longer react in the way that you used to. Your symptoms reduce, or go completely. In my own case, I knew I was well again because I no longer reacted to the heat so badly and could once again cope well with everyday situations.

Other people describe feeling 'different'. They feel that going through their experience has shaped them and changed them in some way –

and generally for the better. For example, they have learnt to think in a way that is more helpful for them, or have made changes for the better in their lives as a result of their anxiety disorder.

Rosie, 40:

I knew I was better because the attacks stopped. But I think of myself as a panic attack sufferer who hasn't had an attack for 12 years. So I'm not complacent. I know it could strike again some time in the future. But I do feel equipped now to prevent it ever getting so bad again.

Gill, 51:

I'm not sure that I'll ever consider myself recovered. I have to accept that I will have good days and bad days, but now I can manage the symptoms and cope with them. I no longer let them take over my life, and that's partly because I asked for help, and through talking to people I realised how common this is. It was such a relief to know that I wasn't going mad, because that was what I thought at first. So for me, this is a process of learning and acceptance.

Phil, 44:

I knew I was better when I forgot to take my medication for several days and hadn't noticed any difference. Now, if I have an attack, I 'manage' my symptoms by breathing and working through it. I haven't taken any medication for two years now, but I still keep it in the drawer like a comfort blanket.

Emma, 25:

I feel like I'm much better than I was. I'm sure that it had been coming on for a long time, and therefore it was a part of me. Going through the whole experience made me change in many ways – in fact the whole thing has been life-changing. I mean, I'm more relaxed about things now. Nothing has to be 'just so' any more. Things don't matter as much. Now, I know I'm OK because I can work without panicking. I couldn't have done this job even a year ago. The whole thing was a horrible, horrible experience, but one that needed to happen, I think.

Sometimes people find that some of their old symptoms emerge from time to time. This is fine and to be expected. Eventually they will get the message that they are redundant, and they'll go away.

Imagine a gang of disruptive teenagers in their final year at school. For months they have been a really bad force in the school. They've terrorised the more vulnerable children, ruined lessons, wreaked havoc in the classrooms and vandalised school property. The school has become gradually weaker and the discipline has dropped considerably as there has been no head teacher in post. The staff are exhausted and many of the students are disillusioned. Little action has been taken to deal with the disruptive element and many of the students are frightened of them. Occasionally the ringleaders are suspended for a day or two, but then they come back and are just as disruptive as before.

After the holidays, when the gang has left, a new head teacher arrives with fresh ideas and an effective approach to bad behaviour and disruption. The school starts to become a much happier, more settled place. Everyone understands what is expected of them and most people are happy to pull together in order to make things work. They accept that it may take time for there to be any noticeable improvement and are prepared to allow and tolerate mistakes and setbacks, as they now know that everything will be much better in the long run.

Every so often, some of the gang members come back. They have nothing to do now that they've left school. They try to get inside to cause havoc for fun, but they cannot. Nobody wants to see them. They split up and each tries get in at different places – round the back, through the art block, in at the changing-room entrance – anywhere where they think they stand a chance. No luck though – they can't get in. Fed up, they go away.

Over the coming months, one or two try desperately to get some attention and disrupt everything again. Sometimes they succeed. For example, one throws a brick through a classroom window. This disrupts the class for the morning, but it's soon fixed. Another time, one of them slashes tyres on bikes and cars. Both of these occurrences are a nuisance. The police have to be called, and it's all a bit unpleasant and unsettling. But then everything returns to normal, with no particular repercussions for the school.

On the whole, no one takes much notice of the former students. Now and then, one or two of them can be seen hovering around outside, desperately trying to attract attention, but no one wants to know. After a while they get bored and go away. In the fullness of time, most of them leave the area. There's no fun to be had around the school any more. They no longer get a response, and no one takes any notice of them any more anyway.

Understand what is happening, accept it and allow it to take its course. There are lessons to be learnt along the way which ultimately will benefit you, as you will know yourself so much better than you did before.

Chapter 8

Hyperventilation and feeling 'unreal' or detached

These are some of the things that people who have had an anxiety disorder have said:

> Everything's affected – relationships, emotions, money, the control you feel you have over your life.
>
> You feel as if you are walking on a tightrope.
>
> It was as if I was trapped in my own mind.
>
> I was me – just not me. A lot of the time I felt the same, but often my feelings and thoughts were not like me.
>
> It's the inability to know what to do, and how to overcome it.
>
> You feel bombarded by your thoughts.
>
> I felt fine in the house and quite lively, like my normal self. But as soon as I went out the feelings came back. So the temptation was to remain in the house all the time.
>
> You feel like you're waiting for your future to start, but when it does, you can't deal with it. You feel as if you are missing the boat.
>
> You start to compare yourself to others. You think: "They can do it but I can't." But it's offensive when others dare to do this too. You

know they're thinking: "X can do it – why can't you?"

Anxiety sucks. It sucks the good balanced stuff from you, and from the people who care about you.

You want to feel warm and fuzzy, not cold and prickly.

The fear of the unknown can make you dishonest. I used to lie to protect myself.

I don't want to grow up. I **am** an adult, but with this anxiety – I just feel so frightened of the responsibility now.

Sometimes I just think that being me is wrong. I think "How would anyone want to spend time with me and care about me if they knew how I feel inside?"

You try to stop thinking but you can't – you feel driven. It's as if you have to go on to the bitter end, like a record that you want to see through to the end, like a compulsion.

Worrying and fretting is like scratching at a wound again and again. Then it gets infected and it gets worse.

It's the shock of realising just how affected you are.

So let's look at some of the most common symptoms:

You may always feel on edge and tense

You may feel calm at certain times, maybe early in the morning, or at night – but then the turmoil starts

Your heart beats too fast, and you feel as if it could burst

Your heart beats too slowly sometimes

Your throat feels blocked, you want to choke

You feel sick. You've been sick

Remember, these are due to an over-worked, over-performing mechanism, called the 'stress response' – that's all

You feel faint. If you've fainted before, you know how horrible it is. So it's hardly surprising that you're likely to be frightened of it happening again

Your stomach is churning, you are constipated or have diarrhoea

Your sleep is disturbed or erratic. You are very tired

You get pins and needles

You get headaches

You sweat at odd times

You shake

You feel giddy and light-headed

You feel that you can't breathe or get enough air (hyperventilation)

You feel 'unreal' and detached from things

Eventually this will find the right balance, and your symptoms will settle

Let's look in particular at these last two symptoms. These can be particularly frightening, because the first makes you feel that you can't breathe, and the second makes you think that you must be going mad.

HYPERVENTILATION

Basically, this means over-breathing. When you breathe quickly and only take in shallow breaths (as if you were panting), the balance of carbon dioxide and oxygen is distorted. We all do this from time to time when we are tense, or have to exert ourselves suddenly. It's part of the fight-or-flight mechanism. The process means that more oxygen is sent to the muscles so that they are ready for action. This is fine and just as it should be, and the body usually readjusts itself back to normal. But too much over-breathing, and for too long, can cause alarming physical symptoms, such as dizziness, feeling as if you can't breathe, assorted pains and discomforts, and tingling or pins and needles.

How you can help yourself immediately

- Know that you will NOT stop breathing or die. You will be OK again soon.
- Carry a paper bag with you and, if you are over-breathing, place it over your nose and mouth. Breathe in and out several times as slowly as you can. This means that you breathe in the same air as you breathe out, which helps to readjust the balance. Now, deep abdominal breathing is often encouraged instead, the idea being that the symptoms subside more naturally. Many people are really glad of a paper bag though.
- *Breathing exercise:* Find something to look at – an object or a place in the distance. Hold your breath for a moment. Now breathe in as slowly and deeply as you can, then breathe out slowly, focusing on that object, and sending your breath to it. Do this a few times, and each time let the breath out last a little longer.

How you can help someone who is hyperventilating

- Speak calmly to them. They are terrified and they need you to reassure them that they will be OK in a minute or two.
- Help them by talking them through the breathing exercise. It can be so reassuring to hear someone helping you. *Your calm, quiet reassuring voice can be their greatest comfort.*

FEELING 'UNREAL' AND DETACHED FROM EVERYTHING

Fran, 26:

I was having an anxiety attack in an art workshop one time. I just wanted to get away. But then someone asked me if I'd like a cup of tea. They didn't seem to have noticed that there was anything the matter with me, yet I imagined that I must seem completely weird, and different to everyone else. I felt detached, as if I was not really

> there. I half expected to faint. My heart was beating so fast and I was intensely aware of each breath in and out. I answered – but my voice didn't seem to belong to me. But as I sipped my tea I gradually began to feel a bit better and my symptoms subsided. I became more fully aware of people around me and I began to feel part of things again.

Derealisation

This is when you might feel as if you are disconnected from everything around you – as if you are going about in a dream. Some people describe this as being like looking through glass or a fog, and feeling 'spaced out'.

Depersonalisation

Or you might feel as if you are detached from your own self – as if you (your thoughts and feelings) are not part of the 'you' that you can see. Some people describe feeling as if they're watching themselves from outside or as if on a TV screen. The technical term for this is Depersonalisation.

Both of these experiences are scary because you worry that you are really losing your mind. But you are not. These sensations are exacerbated by tension and anxiety, but many people experience them at some time in their lives. You can often feel light-headed, dizzy and panicky alongside these. This is horrible, and adds to your anxiety. But remind yourself that it is OK. It's all just part of the process and everything will settle eventually.

How you can help yourself to feel connected

Do something to 'ground' yourself that makes you feel connected to everything again. For example:

- Carry around something that you like, or that is particularly meaningful for you. Something that you can hold and look at, that makes you feel good and that you associate with pleasant things.

- Prepare a meal, cook it and eat it. Notice the colours and textures of the food and the utensils. Feel the water as you wash your hands. Smell the food cooking and listen to the pans bubbling. Enjoy the taste.
- Talk to someone. Really engaging in a conversation with someone so that you fully listen to them and respond, can help to put you in the 'here and now'.
- Do the breathing exercise as for hyperventilation.
- Learn to relax properly, and make a point of practising this for 10-15 minutes every day.

How you can help someone to feel more 'grounded'

- Engage them in a conversation. Make sure you talk about something that interests them. If they are not really interacting with you, that's fine. Just try again later – but avoid overdoing it or they will feel persecuted.
- Encourage them to do something tactile that engages their senses, like have a hot drink or something to eat.
- Encourage them to learn to relax.

Chapter 9

Panic attack or anxiety attack?

For many people, the alarming thing with an anxiety disorder is that all of a sudden, seemingly out of nowhere, comes a completely overwhelming, scary feeling, underpinned by a barrage of thoughts that probably have no basis and are quite irrational. Once this has happened:

1. You worry that it will happen again.
2. You worry about what *might* happen if you feel that way again, and start to imagine the worst-case scenarios. This makes you worry more, and so:
3. You may worry and feel anxious most of the time. But you probably have no idea why.

PANIC ATTACK OR ANXIETY ATTACK?

There is a distinct difference between panic and anxiety. People often assume that they are having a panic attack, but it may actually be an anxiety attack, and it's important to know which it is so that you deal with it in the most appropriate way.

A panic attack

- Comes on very suddenly, and can last for any time between several seconds to about 10 minutes. Sometimes the symptoms come in 'waves' for up to 2 hours.

- A person may experience regular panic attacks, for example several a week or a month – or one or two in a lifetime.
- The symptoms are usually so severe that the person feels as if they are having a heart attack or a stroke, and as if they might die.
- The person often has to do something specific to settle themselves. For example, they might remove themselves from a situation, find a quiet space and, if they feel faint, sit with their head between their legs, or if they are hyperventilating, breathe into a paper bag.
- With a panic attack, people can't usually associate the feeling with anything specific. When they stop and think about it, they can't identify any particular thing that triggered it.
- Panic attacks are unpredictable, and therefore the person who experiences them feels that they have no control over them.

An anxiety attack

- Can come on quickly, but it may have been building over a period of time.
- Although really horrible it is not usually as severe as a panic attack.
- A person will be anxious because of a situation and will feel the need to escape from that. When they do so, the anxiety subsides.

AVOIDING THE ISSUE

Extreme anxiety provokes an abnormal reaction to normal situations. If you know what the cause of this is, you need to deal with the cause and your reaction to it. Otherwise, you may avoid it. All you want to do is feel OK, and if that means avoiding the situation that you think will trigger your discomfort, then of course you will want to do so.

This can be useful as it can give you a chance to recoup, and time to gain a sense of perspective. But eventually you will have to face 'it', whatever that may be. Avoiding something for too long has a negative effect. It means that ultimately you are not dealing with something.

For example, if you keep avoiding paying your bills, do they stop coming? No. Do they pay themselves? No. As you watch the reminder letters pile up, how do you feel as you continue to ignore them? Worried about what the consequences might be? Wouldn't it be better to pay them as soon as you can so that they are out of the way – or at least in instalments, so that you know you are doing something about them?

The same principle applies to avoiding situations where you feel uncomfortable. The situation is unlikely to go away, and the longer you leave it, the less confident you feel about tackling it.

If you continue to avoid the cause:

- You fear it even more
- Your avoidance becomes a habit
- You limit yourself in what you do
- You prevent yourself from testing out whether or not something is really frightening
- You will never show yourself that you can cope
- Your anxiety will continue
- You may do something else which enables you to feel more comfortable, but which may not be the best thing for you. For example, you may use excessive amounts of alcohol or drugs as a way of coping.

There are a range of therapies and techniques that can help you to face your fears, and to take a pro-active approach to dealing with them instead of avoiding them. Currently, Cognitive Behavioural Therapy is one of the favourites. This is because it is a short-term, cost-effective treatment and research has shown that it works. For some people, CBT will not be sufficient. Or it may be that they just do not like it. Many people I have spoken to have found that it has been a help.

CAN ANXIETY WAKEN YOU UP?

"A person's experience may be that they think they are being woken by anxiety, but actually their sleep is just poor. Their sleep is affected because they spend a lot of their time worrying, and the process of that in its own right then disturbs the sleep process. Anxiety is not necessarily going to wake the person up, but they will sleep less, and as soon as they wake up they instantly think anxious thoughts. And, as they are awake, they have more time to worry, so they worry that they aren't sleeping, and so the anxiety gets worse. So a person will sleep less, so be awake more, and therefore have more anxiety." Dr Menzies Schrader, Associate Specialist Psychiatrist.

How you can help yourself to sleep

Do something that enables you to round off the day. Many people go to sleep whilst their mind is still thinking about all the things they've done and have to do. They are trying to shut down their bodies but are not turning off their minds. Therefore:

- Give yourself some kind of bedtime routine that suits you. Small personal rituals can be comforting and stabilising.
- Do some progressive relaxation of your body just before you go to bed.
- Have a relaxing bath.

- Make the bed and the room ready for sleeping; so that means whatever helps you to feel cosy and calm. Some people watch TV, some have the radio on. Some need to have some light. Well, if it helps you to sleep – so be it, but I would suggest that these take the day onward into the night, and really what you need to be doing is switching everything off.

- Avoid heavy meals, alcohol and caffeine for a couple of hours before you go to bed.

- Make sure you have had some physical exercise during the day.

- Give yourself a break – put an end to worrying and fretting about how much or how little sleep you are having. You will survive perfectly well for a while. As your mind and body restores itself, so your sleeping pattern will settle. However, sleep is vital in order for us to function. If a lack of sleep is causing you real and serious problems – for example, if you're nearly falling asleep over machinery, or whilst driving – do seek some treatment.

- Look back over your day in sections. There are various ways that you can do this and the main thing is that you organise your day into progressive sections and 'finish' with each one. For example:

  Draw your day as a cartoon strip. This may sound like a silly idea, especially if you've had a terrible day, but some people find this a really helpful way to end the day. What you do is this: divide a piece of paper (at least A4 in size) into about eight squares – a square for each period of the day, like this:

Early am	Late am	Lunch	Early pm
Late pm	Evening meal	Early evening	Late evening

Now, in each square draw you (this needs to be drawn, not written) doing whatever you did around that time of day. Make this a very simple image – just do stick men if you wish – as this is for your eyes only. Acknowledge any key thoughts and feelings associated with that image, but pay little attention to them. When you have finished, look back over your cartoon strip. Spend a moment or two on each section, from early morning to late evening, and tell yourself that that time has now been and gone and you are finished with it. *And mean it.* Finalise this by drawing a line through it. As you put your pen through the late evening section, say:

"And now I let go of the day. Tomorrow will take care of itself. Now I am ready to drift into a lovely relaxing sleep."

Or you might prefer to watch your day on an imaginary TV screen. Have different pictures for each period of the day as above, starting in the morning, through to the evening. Imagine that you have dials at the bottom of the TV screen so that you can adjust each picture as it comes up. Start with the first picture (early morning). Let the image settle until it is still – like a freeze-frame. Acknowledge key thoughts and feelings but pay little attention to them. Now, using the dials, turn it off. Then go on to the next image – let it settle, and turn it off. Do this until the end of the day and then as you switch off the last image say the words above.

Basically, do this in whatever way you like. Choose time chunks to suit you and just end each one, and then prepare to drift into sleep.

How you can help yourself if you wake up in the night

Get up. If you are over-thinking, get out of bed and do something to distract yourself. The middle of the night seems to be a top time for feeling that you are going mad and that you can't cope. When you wake up, your mind races and churns, and it's horrible. So it is best to get up and move about. Make a drink, do anything to break your thought pattern. For example:

- Get up and get active:

Here's what appears to be a completely whacky exercise but there is a very serious point to it. It is confusing, so you really have to concentrate if you are to do it properly (which means that you focus on something other than your anxious, irrational thoughts). And it engages both sides of your brain, which helps to bring your mind into balance.

- Get a huge sheet of paper and mark it up like the one below.
- Stick it up where you can easily see it.
- Work your way down the sheet, saying each number out loud and, as you do so, complete the action written next to it.
- Repeat the whole exercise a couple of times.

The illustration below is just an example. If you get too used to the sequence, change the numbers and actions around.

Have fun with this, and avoid feeling foolish. After all, how many times have you said you'd do anything to feel better?

1	Right hand to top of head	11	Right hand to Right knee
2	Left elbow to Right knee	12	Left elbow to Right knee
3	Right hand to Right knee	13	Left hand to Right hip
4	Right elbow to Left knee	14	Right elbow to Left knee
5	Left hand to Right shoulder	15	Left hand to Left knee
6	Left hand to top of head	16	Right hand to top of head
7	Right hand to Left hip	17	Left hand to Right shoulder
8	Left hand to Left knee	18	Right hand to Right knee
9	Right hand to Right knee	19	Left elbow to Right knee
10	Left hand to Right shoulder	20	Right elbow to Left knee

- Challenge your negative and anxious irrational thinking. There are lots of tips about this in Chapters 2 and 3
- If you usually write with your right hand, write a few lines with the left one, and vice versa.
- And you can always count sheep. It works for me …

FIRST THING IN THE MORNING

Bill, 42:
When I wake up I always feel dreadful. I have a sense of impending doom. But I know that routine helps so every morning I get straight up, make a cup of tea, shower, and iron my clothes for the day. I've developed a way of dealing with my negative thoughts: for every one that I have, I make myself think of two positive ones. That way, I'm going one better than just counteracting the one negative one.

How you can help yourself start the day

- Get up straight away. If you don't, you are likely to think. Anxious thoughts can kick in immediately, so best to get up and deal with them then, rather than lying in bed (even for a few extra minutes) and letting them grow into monsters.
- Create a morning routine that suits you.
- Have a plan for the day.

BEING ON YOUR OWN

Some people are quite happy in their own company, but others are very uncomfortable about being on their own for any length of time, and this is something to be aware of if you are over-anxious or if you have an anxiety disorder. The fact is that when you are on your own, you are alone with your thoughts. As you know, these can escalate and become quite irrational, and just having someone else around can be reassuring sometimes. Also, they may be able to distract you and help you to focus on something else. If you know that you would be better with someone around you, then perhaps you could take steps to address this. Talk to someone and tell them how you feel. They may be able to suggest a way forward.

Don, 31:
Don had made a mistake in business and was unable to let the memory of it go. He was over-anxious and fearful a great deal of the time, but never more so than when he was by himself, when his thoughts became completely irrational and he constantly blamed himself for ruining his family's life. This began to knock his confidence and self-esteem dreadfully. It got so out of hand that he told himself that he 'couldn't handle' being by himself for more than about an hour. The truth is, he was frightened of his own thoughts and feelings.

Nina, 27:
Nina felt unable to settle every time her partner went out. She described feeling

"Not in control. I like having the company, and having someone to care for and talk to." In therapy it transpired that it was not so much the fact that she was alone that bothered her as the fear of the feelings that she might experience. She had once had a panic attack when she was by herself in the house. She was really frightened that this might happen again while she was on her own and that there would be no one to look after her.

The moment you grasp the concept of **Understand, Accept, Allow** you put a solid foundation in place which enables the healing process to begin. This is because there is no need to keep hold of all those worries and fears now. They're redundant. You now know what's going on, and you know that eventually you will feel better. Avoid thinking:

"*Yes but* … it's not like that for me." Or "*But* I can't do that because

…" Thoughts like those are just excuses. Remember that I have been through an anxiety disorder myself and I know how overwhelming the symptoms can be. There is a tremendous urge to fight how you feel and to think that you are insane. But you are not. You are going to be OK.

Chapter 10

People's stories

PEOPLE'S STORIES

Here are some stories from people who have had anxiety disorders.

Dawn, 26:

I had my first symptoms when I was 15, at school, around the time my stepfather died. I was sick at the end of a science lesson – but not in front of anyone else. I just thought I was ill and that it would pass. The symptoms didn't go away though. It was horrendous – I'd feel hot, sick, shaky, my heart would race and my breathing changed. I felt that I had to get out of the situation. Initially I avoided going to school or going out in general. I just stayed at home in my room. I did get through though, and completed my exams.

I used to be dismissed as neurotic sometimes, and that was hurtful. But now I know that it was just that people didn't understand. I've been offered medication a couple of times but I chose not to take it, and the doctor gave me a booklet to read on anxiety and panic. I got support and counselling through a work support line and now I know how to challenge my thoughts when they get out of hand, which helps. I've learnt to breathe through an attack and to just wait until it passes. For example, if I have an attack in the supermarket I just stay there and walk around until the feeling has subsided. And I set small goals for myself too. I find this all helps me to feel in control.

Now, I have far less frequent attacks and can go for quite a long period without one. I know I'm hugely better because I suggest to others that we do things like go out for a meal, or the theatre, and I am happy to go. But I always make sure I know where the exits are and where the loo is. And I would prefer to sit at the end of a row or near an exit if possible.

Sunita, 24:
The whole thing lasted for about two years. I first realised something was wrong near the beginning of my second year at university, when I had a lecture and felt I couldn't breathe and wanted to be sick. I had to leave the room.

I just had the feeling that I was on my own in this huge city. I felt that I'd moved out of home and couldn't allow myself to have support because I was supposed to be an adult and had to deal with it all myself. I wouldn't allow myself to be homesick. So what started it was probably the realisation that "I can't deal with this myself and I'm scared".

At first I thought I was going crazy and felt very, very alone. I had this feeling that I was suddenly seeing the world as it really is and I felt I couldn't bear to live with it and myself as they really are. It was as if I'd seen a gaping hole in the universe. One of the major things for me was realising things about myself and blowing them out of all proportion and thinking: "How can I live with myself when I'm like this?" and "I'm never going to find anyone who understands how I feel and who can like me when I tell them what I'm like. Because no one else will be as insane as I am." I felt like I was living a lie because I couldn't tell anyone how I really felt.

But then I did go for help – the doctor and counsellors. They all told me I wasn't mad, so my understanding about the whole thing changed. I allowed myself to panic and I accepted that nothing bad was going to happen. I had six sessions of one-to-one CBT and read a couple of books about anxiety, which helped. I also listened to relaxation CDs each night. And I had good family support. And I think the fact that I allowed myself to feel proud of doing small things was important for me. I made myself see that they were an achievement and took care not to belittle them. Also, I learnt to stop doing things that I felt I 'should' be doing.

Rebecca, 65:
Rebecca had her first anxiety attack when her mother died. She described feeling as if she'd been "hit in the solar plexus and throat". Fifty years later she was still plagued by anxiety and this had continued throughout her busy life. Now a widow, she felt very much on her own. She described feeling worse in the mornings when sometimes she'd want to be sick. "Something within me is creating an insecurity. It can play havoc with my days and how I feel. Anxiety rips my innards out. It can be about something that I need to sort out – like arranging for a plumber to come, or getting someone to fix the window. It just worries me so much. It's ridiculous. But when I've organised it I feel so much better. Doing stuff takes away the level of worry somehow."

Declan, 40:
When I came out of prison I found going in crowds of people was scary. I felt overwhelmed for months. I suppose I'd been out of the loop for a long time and I'd lost my confidence.

But I've always been insular – kept my thoughts and emotions to myself all my life. When I was a kid it was just easier not to talk about how I felt about things. I'd put up guards and shields. It can be uncomfortable taking them down, and for a long time I didn't want counselling or anything because I was frightened of emerging like a jelly at the end. I'm on my own and I used to think "Who'll pick up the pieces?" Trying to handle your thoughts and feelings on your own is difficult. It's too much. You need someone to steer. I realised that, when I eventually did see a counsellor.

I used to see the whole process like a staircase with different landings where you get off at various ones and open doors. It really helped. Being able to talk about stuff I'd kept buried for so long gave me a platform for going forward. It's helped me to deal with day-to-day things and with larger issues. I don't get anxious among people and crowds now at all.

Claire, 40:
I've had two bouts of real anxiety and panic attacks. The first was when I was 22. The second time I was 34 and I recognised the symptoms almost instantly, which was a big help.

It was absolutely terrifying. Waves of adrenalin constantly, shakiness, palpitations, and then the actual panic attacks themselves. The first time round they became so frequent I couldn't count them – there was barely a break between them. I had trouble breathing and was convinced I was dying.

I think I knew it was a panic attack but I had no previous experience and couldn't believe anyone else had ever experienced anything so extreme. I had no idea how common it is, because most people just didn't talk about it. So I thought I was alone and that I had a real mental health problem. But once I admitted it, various people said, "I've had panic attacks before," which was incredibly reassuring. Some of them were very supportive. Up to that point I was sure the panic attacks would kill me, and if they didn't I'd be got by one of the many hypochondriac illnesses I was suddenly convinced I had. I became completely self-obsessed and the attacks dominated my life.

During both periods when I had these attacks, I'd felt trapped in my life. Situations were outside my control – and though I didn't realise it at the time, I think this lack of control was a huge factor for me. The first time, I felt trapped in my job – I'd signed a fixed term contract. But I did leave, and this helped. I think that gave me the control back. The second time round I was having medical tests. The waiting times for appointments seemed to drag on for ever and I was also very stressed. I think I just couldn't cope with the sheer frustration as well as the lack of control.

The first time I had these attacks I had no idea what to do. The doctor gave me a Valium which helped for a few hours but then the symptoms just came straight back. Eventually it was my uncle who helped, because he'd been there himself. He taught me to:

- Breathe into a paper bag when I was hyperventilating.
- Use positive affirmations. He told me not to expect a result for weeks but to stick with it. He taught me to recognise the earliest possible stage of an attack and go through the affirmations then, rather than waiting until it was in full swing. So I'd tell myself things like: "You can get through this. You are perfectly well and healthy and this will pass. You are getting better every day." This was really empowering. For the first time, I was able to feel that I could deal with my panic attacks myself. The affirmations worked straight away, and from that point I knew I'd be better able to cope if the panic attacks recurred.

The second time around I knew what was going on instantly. Within days I saw my GP, who was much more helpful than the doctor I'd seen 12 years before, and he put me on a short course of beta-blockers. I took them for a week and then just occasionally when I needed them. Within about three weeks the whole episode was over, whereas the first time round it had gone on for months. The fact that I'd caught my symptoms so early, and had done something about it, made an enormous difference.

Ben, 30:

My thing is public speaking. It started years ago when I had to give a presentation for work. For about a month before, I couldn't think of anything else. I wasn't scared, just embarrassed and nervous. I thought it must be really obvious to everyone else. I got through it by speaking fast and sitting down as quickly as I could. Then I avoided doing any more for as long as I could. I think I built up an irrational fear, because it gradually got worse.

I'd get a feeling of everything closing in on me, like I was going in on myself. My legs felt like they were going to give way. My breathing would get shallow and fast and I'd feel like I wouldn't be able to speak. My voice would shake, I'd shake, and my fingertips would go absolutely white. It felt like impending doom. I'd have palpitations and feel as if I could faint. Actually, I still get the symptoms. I know my trigger. It's when I know I have to speak out in public. Then I work myself up. I think things like "What if they ask me to write something down and I can't because I'm shaking?" and "What if I can't speak and they can see that I'm really shaky?" and "Why can't I be normal?" I torture myself, thinking about what's going to happen. The whole thing only lasts for about two minutes. It peaks, and then I can't concentrate on anything for a while after.

But I've learnt how to deal with it now. For example, I stop my thinking by pushing thoughts out as they come into my head, and I challenge them and rationalise them. Also I do other things to distract myself, such as exercise. And I relax more. I know I'm getting better because each time I've had to do a presentation at work I've been less nervous. I'm gradually getting more used to it now. But a couple of times I've felt more than usual that it's building up again. I don't want it to be a problem again. It's the initial thing – that fear. Sometimes I don't feel strong enough to get through that. I'll think "I can't do it this time."

Usually though, I feel like I can overcome it, which is good. I've learnt that I'm stronger than I think I am, because I know that a lot of people would just say "I'm not doing it, and that's it," but I persevere. And I do put too much pressure on myself. I don't like everyone's focus on me. I've never liked that. People don't actually appreciate how awful I feel, because I laugh it off.

I find that having other people as a back-up helps me to do it, so they could take over if necessary. I know I won't always need that, but it helps at the moment. Also, I looked up my symptoms and realised that this happens sometimes. I had some hypnotherapy, which helped a lot, and acupuncture. And I've learnt to face the fear, because I'd always avoided it. So what I do now is, if I feel like I'm going to faint, I've stood up, felt it, and then it subsided. That's helped – just knowing that the feeling would go has helped. What definitely doesn't help is putting pressure on myself. Telling myself "I've got to do it" and "This is ridiculous, you should be able to do this" makes me feel worse.

Chapter 11

How to help yourself

Jenna, 28:

People need to know that having an anxiety disorder is not the end of the world. It really isn't. It feels like it at the time, but it gets better, and you can learn to manage it until it goes.

When your anxiety is out of control, you can spend a large proportion of your time looking for potential dangers and threats, and imagining the effect they could have on you. These become the focus of your time, attention and energy. So you develop unhelpful patterns of thinking. For example:

- You are likely to see difficulties and dangers for yourself where none exist.
- You might expect the worst to happen in any scenario and think that some things are far worse than they really are.
- You will probably jump to conclusions about all sorts of things.

So of course you worry, which raises your anxiety - and the reaction to this (the stress response) becomes a normal and familiar state for you. In fact, you are frightened of the feelings themselves. So you need to break this pattern.

Here are some great ways to help yourself to do that:

LEARN TO RELAX

This is the key self-help tool that pops up in all therapies and treatments. A relaxed body makes for a relaxed mind. You know that your symptoms are caused by extra chemicals flooding your body to help you to cope with an emergency. When you consciously relax your body, this sends feedback to the brain that it no longer needs to be ready for action. It's as if your relaxed body tells the brain:

"Everything is fine here and relaxed, so we don't need to fight or fly at the moment."

For many people, relaxing properly can be one of the most tricky things to do. It's not the same as flopping in front of the TV or doing some other activity. This is progressive relaxation, whereby you concentrate on each separate part of your body and allow it to relax – bit by bit. You may already be familiar with this, but if you are not, you need to give yourself time to discover how it works. And it does work. Some people are able to do this immediately but you may well find it takes a while. You'll probably twitch and wriggle around trying to get comfortable, and your mind might flatly refuse to take any notice of what you are telling it to do. In fact, when you are in the midst of your symptoms, any thoughts of relaxation can seem impossible. This is absolutely fine. Just keep practising.

You may also be surprised by your emotional response as you learn to relax. For example, you might cry. One of the reasons for this is that as you release the tension in your muscles for the first time you may trigger old reactions and experiences, which have been carried around in your body for a long time. You may have no idea why you are crying – and that's fine. It's just a release, and, if it does happen, it may not do so for quite some time as you start to learn a new pattern of releasing and relaxing.

There are many recorded relaxation tapes and CDs available and I would really recommend that you invest in one, because being talked through the process will help you to focus. Be sure however that it is a progressive relaxation of your body. Below is an outline of the method. You could record yourself, or ask someone to read a relaxation process for you. If this is what you choose, you will need to flesh out what is written below for each part of your body, like this: "Take your attention to your toes. Tense them – feel the tension, and relax them. Let them go."

This process will take about 15 to 20 minutes and you need to be quiet and undisturbed, and comfortable and warm:

- Lie down or sit in a chair.
- Close your eyes. This is important as it frees you from extra distractions
- Listen to the sounds around you. Just be aware of the myriad sounds in your environment. First notice the sounds *outside* the building.
- After a couple of moments, take your attention to the sounds *inside* the building or the room you are in. Just focus on them for a few moments.
- Then listen to the sounds of your own body and your breathing.
- Take your attention to each part of your body, *slowly* tensing and then relaxing each in turn. Start with your toes, then feet, ankles, lower legs, upper legs, buttocks, torso, fingers, arms, shoulders, neck, back of head, top of head, forehead, eyelids, cheeks, nose, jaw, and tongue.
- Tense each part – and let it go. Let each part of your body flop and relax. Take your time, there's no rush.
- Let your breath flow gently in and out of your body.
- Eventually you will become relaxed and still.

- You might like to go a stage further and imagine yourself in a beautiful and relaxing place. Stay there for a few minutes.
- When you are ready, stretch – and open your eyes. Allow yourself to come round *slowly.*
- *Slowly* sit up (if you are lying down). Keep in the moment – let the relaxed feeling stay with you for as long as you can.

It doesn't really matter how you learn to relax, as long as you build up an awareness of the sensations. Systematically tensing and relaxing your muscles is a great way as it helps to increase you own body-awareness and it sends the right messages to your already over-stressed system.

Gradually you will find that you can become relaxed quite quickly, in all sorts of situations, such as when you're sitting at your desk or doing the washing up. Be aware of unnecessary tension in your body. Tell yourself to relax and let go.

If you're in distress, you need to de- stress.
The more you de-stress, the more you stress less.

THINK IN A POSITIVE WAY

One of the finest things that you can do for yourself, and the one that will bring about the most profound change, is to change the way you think about the situation and to think positively. This will help you to face situations that you have found challenging.

Why thinking positively is important:

- Language is your most powerful tool. The way that you communicate with yourself and with others has an impact on how you think, feel and behave. Therefore it is an essential part of your life and the lives of those around you.

- Your 'self talk' – what you tell yourself in your head, is hugely important because it has a real effect on you. So it's important to understand something of how the mind works. Then you can make your self talk work for you.

Basically, there are two parts to the mind: the conscious and the subconscious. Many therapists use the term 'unconscious' instead of 'subconscious,' and many describe the workings of the mind in much more detail. The following is a simplistic explanation and, in my opinion, it's all you need:

Your conscious mind:
This is the part of your mind that you think with. You know, through your conscious mind, that you are aware and in the present. It is the reasoning part of your mind – the part that makes decisions and choices. It acts as a filter to thoughts and suggestions, deciding where to place them or whether to get rid of them. When a thought or suggestion is accepted, the information filters into the subconscious.

Your subconscious mind:
The subconscious then organises the information. It's a container for your thoughts and feelings. It is amazing, and it works incredibly hard. This is the part of the mind that deals with all the automatic workings of your body, such as your heartbeat and your breathing. So it works while you are awake and asleep. It never stops.

The subconscious takes orders from the conscious mind. It is extremely obedient and believes that what it is told is true. It doesn't discriminate and it has absolutely no sense of humour. Once the subconscious accepts an idea it starts to implement it. It doesn't care whether it is a good or a bad idea – it's only interested in obeying what the conscious has told it to do. Then the really hard work starts. The subconscious makes sure that the suggestion or idea is carried out and it creates the right conditions for this to happen.

For example, if you have constantly negative or anxious thoughts, and you repeat them often enough, they will filter into your subconscious. It will accept these as the truth. It will then create an environment where these can take over. Similarly, when your thoughts are repeatedly positive, **and you really believe them**, your subconscious works to make sure that these flourish and you thrive.

Imagine that as an experiment you plant two saplings side by side. You give the first one fertiliser from a packet called 'Worry, Fear and Misery'. This is full of poison. You give the other sapling 'Bright and Optimistic' fertiliser, which you know is really beneficial. The fertilisers filter through the top layers of soil down to where the saplings' roots are. Every now and then you top up their water with a little more fertiliser from their corresponding packets.

In the fullness of time you go to look at the trees and guess what? The tree that was fertilised with 'Worry, Fear and Misery' is stunted and small. Its branches have shrivelled and twisted. The ground around it is bare and dry.

The tree that was fed with 'Bright and Optimistic' has really grown. Its branches are strong and far-reaching. It is covered in healthy green leaves. People gravitate towards it because it attracts them and it is a good place to be.

You decide to help the stunted tree and start feeding it with 'Bright and Optimistic'. After a short time you notice that the tree is more upright. Its branches are straightening out and they are stronger. As time goes on it becomes more and more like the other tree. Now it, too, is a good place to be. At any point you can save the withered tree by feeding it with good fertiliser.

At any point you can change your thinking by feeding your mind with positive self talk and replacing negative and anxious thoughts with positive ones. It's really important that you do this *and that you fully believe those thoughts.* This will help you to think differently about the things that have been bothering you, and about the way you have been reacting to them. It will send a very powerful message to your subconscious that there is no need to be fearful any more. It will let your whole system know that you're the boss, you're in control, and you're not standing for any more nonsense.

So, you might think things like:

I know that no harm will come to me. I understand what my anxiety is, and I am now learning to keep calm and relaxed.

I understand what is happening and I accept this, because I am confident that I am now healing and becoming well.

Now, I am able to keep calm and relaxed.

Now, I have nothing to fear from ...

I trust myself to respond calmly to all situations.

I know that I am well. I know that my whole being is working perfectly.

I know this can be tricky to do at first. When you feel so down, and so frightened, you can't be bothered to speak sometimes, let alone be positive. But the more you do it, the easier it gets. Just practise. You are simply replacing an unhelpful habit with a really good one.

TAKE TIME TO BREATHE:

Breathing is automatic and you may usually pay little attention to it. So just notice – when you are tense, do you:

- Breathe in small, shallow breaths?
- Breathe more quickly?
- Hold your breath for short periods?

Become aware of how you breathe so that you can make it work for you more effectively. Taking the time to breathe deeply will slow you down and enable you to become calmer when you are tense and anxious. Here are three breathing exercises to practise:

1 Taking control

Be aware that when you take tense, shallow breaths, you do not fill your lungs properly with air and tend to breathe with the top half of your chest. What will help you to become calmer is to be able to breathe more deeply and fully, and fill your lungs with air. At first this can be easiest to do when you are lying down. So:

- Lie down comfortably, on your back. (This is great to do after a conscious relaxation.)
- Have a good stretch.
- Place one or both hands on your navel.
- Just be aware of your breath – in and out of your nostrils. Notice what happens to your hand. As you breathe in, the idea is that the general area of your body around and above your navel should gently rise and expand as you fill your lungs with air. It should fall as you breathe out. If it doesn't – no matter. It will eventually, especially if you mentally 'send' the breath down there as you breathe in.
- Imagine that you have a small feather just above your lips.
- Take a good breath in, and as you breathe out, gently blow that imaginary feather up to the ceiling (or the sky if you are outside). It doesn't matter if it doesn't go as far as you want it to.
- Do this a few times, and each time send the feather a little further until it gets to wherever you want it to go.

Enjoy doing this. It's not a competition or a punishment. The great thing is that you are in control of your breathing whilst you do the exercise. You will find that with each breath your breathing becomes deeper and more full.

- When you feel ready, try doing this standing up. You won't need a feather now. Just send your breath forwards to a chosen spot in front of you. You will find this is quite a different sensation.
- You can play with this, sending your breath to different places – inside the room, to a tree or a building outside, through a cloud – wherever you like. Your breath will just get fuller and deeper as you do so.
- Practise this a few times a day so that breathing deeply becomes more natural to you.

2 Feel connected

This is a good exercise and particularly useful if you feel 'unreal' or detached from everything:

- Stand still, in bare feet or flat shoes. Feel the solid floor or ground underneath you, supporting you.
- Place your hands on your abdomen.
- Breathe out first, and pause.
- Now take a slow deep breath and imagine it going right down into your abdomen.
- Pause, and then *slowly* breathe out, making a slight noise in the back of your throat like a sigh as your release the breath.
- Take as long as you need, and get rid of all the rest of the air by pulling in your stomach.
- Try this two or three times and you'll notice how much deeper each breath in becomes.

This is a great way of taking control of your breathing, which in turn helps you to feel connected again. Be gentle with yourself though. It doesn't matter if you can't do this at first – it's just a good technique to practise. And take care not to overdo it because you may feel slightly dizzy if you do.

3 In short, out long

This is another good calming technique to practise. The idea is that the breath out is always longer than the breath in.

- Stand still, in bare feet or flat shoes. Feel the solid floor or ground underneath you, supporting you.
- Place your hands on your abdomen.
- Breathe out first, and pause.
- Breathe in while you count to five. Synchronise your breath with the count so that, as you get to the number five, you've taken in all the breath you can.
- Breathe out while you count to seven. Again, synchronise your breath with the count so that, as you reach number seven, you get rid of all of the air.
- Do this several times and then lengthen each breath out, to the count of nine, 11 and so on. Make sure you are comfortable and don't overdo it.

All these exercises help you to take back control by focusing on your breathing, instead of focusing on your fearful and anxious thoughts.

Breathless people are tense people

CHOOSE TO GO WITH THE FLOW

Know that your symptoms will pass. So just accept them (no matter how uncomfortable they are) and let them happen. You may find it helps to imagine yourself drifting gently through a situation without resistance of any kind. So for example, if you have to go into a room full of people just imagine you are drifting through the door and in amongst them. If the unpleasant feelings that you associate with this come up – let them. They won't harm you. Drift through them, because they will pass. You know that now. You can drift about in the room, doing whatever you need to do, and when you are finished you simply drift out again. Tell yourself:

"I'll just drift through this and go with the flow, and nobody need ever know."

There is something very soothing about allowing yourself to drift when you feel apprehensive and scared. And it gives you a great feeling of being in control, because you aren't *aimlessly* drifting. You're *choosing* to do so.

CHALLENGE YOUR ANXIOUS, IRRATIONAL THOUGHTS

This has been covered in some detail in Chapters 2 and 3. A great addition to this is to invest in a digital voice recorder and carry it with you:

- It can be useful to say your worried, anxious thoughts into a voice recorder, as you think them. Later, when you feel calmer, you can play them back and even write them down. This can be helpful because you then will have a record of *exactly* what you thought at the time and, more importantly, *how often you think the same kind of things.* This can help you to be really clear so that you can work out excellent challenges and reframe the thoughts positively. Practise your challenge and positive reframes. Then you can use them when you need to.

Some digital voice recorders also have a music recording facility, which means that you can use your favourite music to distract you too. And of course some mobile phones have every facility available.

Whatever you use, it's great to have something small that you can carry around with you at all times.

When you are playing back your recording, just notice: do you have a tendency to make vast assumptions about people or situations? If so, you need to challenge this. For example, your assumption might be:

"People don't contact me because they think I'm odd." Challenge this by:

- Looking for the evidence.

  Ask yourself:
  "Where's the evidence? How do I know for sure that this is what they think? What proof have I got?"

- Thinking of how many other explanations there could be for something.

  Ask yourself:
  "What other explanation might there be for their not contacting me? Are they ill or too busy? Has their phone broken?"

LESSEN THE PRESSURE

- If you know that you put great pressure on yourself to achieve highly in various areas of your life – let it go.
- If other people have high expectations of you and what you can achieve, prepare to disappoint them.
- Give yourself a break. As an adult, you have a choice about what you do and do not do. If you are highly stressed and anxious, or if you have an anxiety disorder, now is definitely not the time to push yourself to the limit.
- So challenge your irrational 'I should', and 'I must'-type thoughts, and positively reframe them into something more helpful for you.

DISTRACT YOURSELF

If you feel your thoughts are getting out of hand – think about something else. This can be easier said than done when your thoughts are racing, or when you are over-analysing and scared. So have a couple of things to hand that will distract you and take you away from your thoughts, such as the phone number of someone you can call to chat to, or something that you can do to shift the focus of your attention to something more helpful. For example, listen to some music or an audio CD, go for a walk, do some exercise.

CREATIVE VISUALISATION

This is a good way to distract yourself and to help yourself to have a mental break. It's great to do when you have just done some conscious relaxation:

- Take some time to discover your own special place – somewhere that you love, that is good, and where you feel safe and at peace. Create your own sanctuary in your mind. This may be somewhere that you know or somewhere that you invent. For example:

  A beach with smooth white sand
  A fabulous garden with flowers and trees
  A wood with a stream
  A cool and sunny ski slope
  A wonderful room
  A marble temple

- Imagine the place you've chosen and be aware of it in as much detail as possible. Notice the climate, the colours, the sounds, scents and tastes. Make it just right for *you.* This is your own special sanctuary.
- Give yourself time to really experience this place. Really 'be' there.
- When you're satisfied that it is the best that it can be, just notice

what stands out for you. Is there some aspect of it that you'll remember above everything else? You can use this to trigger the memory of this place again and to fix you into it.

- Once you've really got it, you'll get it again and be able to return there easily.

With practice you can put yourself right back there in seconds – so it can help to calm you and provide a different focus when you are feeling overwhelmed by your symptoms.

KEEP OCCUPIED

It's important to acknowledge and accept your uncomfortable feelings as being part of the process. However, if you give them too much attention they will love it and thrive. So keep yourself occupied, as every time you think about your fear it enables it to grow. When you are fully engaged in an activity or an interesting conversation you help yourself to keep calm. Giving yourself one definite thing to do helps.

SET YOURSELF ACHIEVABLE TASKS

- Some people find that planning out their day is useful. This means that they have less spare time to dwell on what might or might not happen. Avoid overdoing it though. Make sure that you include some exercise and relaxation time.
- Allow yourself 'worry space'. Some people find that planning a specific block of time in which to explore their worried, anxious, irrational and fearful thoughts (about 15 minutes) works for them. The idea is to cram all your intrusive thoughts into this time and challenge them as you go along. As other fears and anxieties pop up throughout the day, you decide to save them for the 'worry space'. This is a good idea as it means that you put mental boundaries in place, and ultimately you take control. Try it, and see what you think. It's an idea that could work well for you.

- Prioritise on paper. Make a list of what needs doing today, what can wait until tomorrow, and what can wait for a while. The 'today' list needs to be done like this:

  - Make sure the first item is something that you enjoy.
  - The next item should be something that you can do really quickly.
  - The third item should be something that you've already started.

This is a great trick because you feel that you're making progress straight away.

After this, prioritise by doing *first* the thing you like least, and tick each item off as you go. Give yourself plenty of time and avoid beating yourself up if you don't do what you had hoped. It's OK. Remember this is all part of a process.

CHANGE POSITION OR DO SOMETHING ELSE

This can have an amazing affect. For example, if you are sitting or lying down and you are thinking about how you feel, how long is it before you have thought yourself into an anxious state? I have watched people do this sometimes – sitting quietly, head down looking at their hands – everything going downwards and inwards, including their thoughts. Or someone lying back, staring at the ceiling – thinking about how bad they feel. But when those people got up and moved, things changed. They took control and became more powerful. When they spoke, they sounded decisive and strong.

So if you notice that you are thinking unhelpfully, do something else. Get up and move. Make a cup of tea. Combine this with a few positive statements to yourself, and you regain control.

Through making these changes, your mind and body gradually learn a new pattern. They learn not to respond in the old way to the triggers. The sensations become less intense until one day, you will hardly remember them. **They really do become just a memory.**

It can take quite some time to adjust to becoming less stressed and fearful, when you have been so for a long time. The advice generally is to take small steps, not to attempt giant leaps.

PEOPLE TO SUPPORT YOU

You need to feel supported. There is no reason for you to struggle through this on your own. So do ask for help, even though this is something that may not come easily to you. You do need to talk to someone, and have a person who is there for you when you need them. If you do not have a trusted family member or friend, you could ask the doctor what he or she would advise, and if you get in touch with some of the mental health organisations they may be able to suggest a way forward. Also, the mental health help lines are fantastic. It is such a relief to be able to pick up the phone and hear a calm, helpful, non-judgemental voice at the other end.

EXERCISE AND DIET

Make sure that you get sufficient exercise and that you eat properly and regularly. You need to look after yourself. If you are not hungry, that's fine – just make sure you eat small, nutritious snacks. Avoid too much caffeine, which stimulates the nervous system, and alcohol, which depresses it. Your nervous system needs to settle itself and large quantities of these won't help.

DO WHAT IT TAKES TO REGAIN CONTROL

You want to feel in control of your life again, and secure. Sometimes there is little you can do to change a situation, but what you can do is manage the way you think and feel about it. Though avoiding whatever is the cause or trigger for your symptoms is not ultimately helpful, I think that in the short term it can be. Sometimes you just need some time out, and some support. For example, it's noble and good to have a strong work ethic, but at what cost to yourself do you struggle on regardless? I'm not suggesting that anyone should skive or be lazy, but so many people feel too pressured in their place of work, and this isn't healthy. You need time to recoup and rest. So have it. No one is indispensable.

KEEP A RECORD

It can be useful to keep a daily record of how you are doing throughout the day. You could write this or use a voice recorder – but it would be useful to have a written transcript for reference at a later date.

Note the following, and rate how severe your symptoms were on a scale from 1–10, one being calm and 10 being real panic:

- Date and time.
- What the situation was that brought on your symptoms.
- How severe your symptoms were.
- What you thought, felt and did.
- Mention the good times too, and anything specifically related to these.

You might like to record it like this. Keep it simple to start with:

Date and time	Situation	Symptom severity 1–10	Thoughts/feelings/ behaviour	Good things and why

Keep this with you and add to it as soon as you can after the symptoms occur, while you remember the details. This can help you to recognise patterns so that, for example, you may find that you are more, or less, affected at certain times of day. It also provides a useful record for a therapist.

Chapter 12

When someone you know has an anxiety disorder

You may have no idea that someone has an anxiety disorder, because:

- You may not be able to tell from how a person looks. They may look wonderful, and serene and content. Inside they might feel like a quivering jelly in turmoil.
- They have probably not told you. This is because not only are they frightened and confused about what is happening to them, but also because they may be embarrassed. There is still a stigma attached to any kind of mental illness or disorder.

One young woman had a panic attack on the Underground. The only way her friend realised what was happening was because she had been through a similar experience herself and she wanted to do what she could to help. Later the young woman reluctantly admitted that this is what had happened, but she refused to discuss it and just smoothed over it saying: "Oh I used to get them years ago." It was never mentioned again

- They may not have told you because they may be deeply fearful that you will then talk about them to someone else.

A well-known member of a rock band was secretly terrified to go on stage. He was frightened of the responsibility of having to deliver a set each night and this fear began to take over and spoil his life. He didn't tell anyone, but to the rest of the group he appeared moody and distant. He drank too much and used drugs extensively to help him to cope, but this just made him feel paranoid. Underneath, he felt pathetic. He craved to be left alone and to be tranquil and at peace. But he said that the most humiliating thing was knowing that his friends were talking about him behind his back because he was not coping.

- You may mistake their behaviour for something else.

One day I got onto an aeroplane and walked past a man who had taken an aisle seat near the front. "How selfish," I thought. "Choosing the best seat for himself. How are other people supposed to climb over him into their seats?" Later, I remembered that when I was going through my anxiety period I used to panic when I was in confined spaces. I rather sheepishly realised that perhaps he did too, and was simply managing his anxiety in the best way that he could.

Paul, 28:
My supervisor said "You're not pulling your weight." That really knocked me for six because I was doing my best not to appear lazy or anything. But I just couldn't bear being in that room with everyone else."

Karen, 22:
I used to love going out with my friends until I became like this. But I've had to make excuses since I've felt so awful. I've told them about my anxiety, but I don't think any of them really understand at all. They've gradually stopped telling me about things that they're doing, and I asked my closest friend why. "It's just that you're unreliable," she said. That really hurt.

The experience of an anxiety disorder is very intense, and very unpleasant. However, someone with an anxiety disorder can provoke a range of thoughts and emotions in those that care about them.

Their behaviour can appear intensely irritating. Some people constantly seek reassurance. Some clam up and won't tell you why.

Elements of anxiety can manifest in different ways, all of which can drive others to distraction:

- The person can become over-organised and obsessive, believing that everything has to go a certain way, and be 'just so'.
- On the other hand, the person might respond the opposite way and become disorganised and chaotic.
- They may blame other people and situations for how they feel. For example, they might think:

"*I can't go out because it will make me anxious.*" When really what they need to do is think:

"*I can go out because I'm in control. If I get anxious, I can deal with it using various techniques.*"

'Just get on with it and don't fuss'

Some people think that to carry on regardless, and to 'get on and do' is the right attitude. But it's not – at least until a diagnosis has been made. For example, if the cause of, or the trigger for, the anxiety is likely to go of its own accord, then it might be appropriate to 'just get on with it' and keep going. But if it's not likely to go away, then to keep on going is not going to help. This becomes a way to avoid dealing with the issue.

Some of this attitude is to do with the stigma attached to any form of mental illness or disorder. There is a general belief that mental illness or disorder carries with it a loss of personal control. People fear this, as personal control is an important social value.

If people see that someone has lost personal control, they tend to be a bit wary. Many are empathic and supportive but some withdraw from the person, simply because they don't understand. Many people have never experienced the symptoms themselves, therefore they have absolutely no idea how it feels and how debilitating an anxiety disorder can be. Perhaps they might think that this is not something that is likely to happen to them – until it does.

Everyone should understand something of anxiety and depression

HOW WELL DO YOU KNOW THE PERSON?

Someone who has severe anxiety or an anxiety disorder may appear to be incredibly selfish. But this is because they are overwhelmed by their symptoms and are trying to cope with them in the best way that they can. Others may be impatient with them because they don't understand what they are going through.

Friends and acquaintances

> **Joe, 25:**
> Some friends were great and really understanding, but some were not. They didn't understand at all, and kept saying the wrong things. Also, some of my family – though they tried to understand, they just managed to say the wrong things too, which made me feel stupid and disrespected, and would leave me questioning my sanity again.

One of the fears that the individual will have is that people that they know, like and respect are talking about them behind their back. They worry that they are being thought of as 'odd', 'weird', 'moody', 'crazy', 'unreliable', 'lazy', 'ill-and-need-to-see-the-doctor', plus a range of other labels. One of their greatest fears may be that they could actually be going mad, or that they are really ill. Therefore, if you are a friend or acquaintance of someone who has an anxiety disorder, you will help them much more if you show them support and understanding and avoid gossiping about them.

You may feel uneasy because you don't know what to do. So you may be tempted to withdraw from the person. Whilst you may feel more comfortable doing this, you're not helping the person with the anxiety disorder. They don't want to be ostracised. They still want to be a part of things and to feel included and wanted – it's just that they find some things tricky because of their symptoms. So it is important that you are thoughtful and considerate. Be honest with them about how you feel, but be realistic. Show them that you are making an effort and not dismissing them as 'odd' or 'ill'. They will appreciate this – even though they may not say so.

Those who are closest

All those who are close to the person are likely to be affected in some way. All relationships are unique, and for some it can be tricky to know exactly what your role is. For example, siblings in the family can get caught in the middle, in a sort of no-man's land.

> **Portia, 17, whose sister, 19 developed GAD:**
> I knew there was something wrong because she kept feeling sick and wanting reassurance all the time. I'd think: "For God's sake – just get on with it. People feel sick a lot of the time, but it happens."
>
> Mum told me what was the matter with her, and I understood, because it was a bit like depression. Our dad had had depression and it was awful being around him then, so I used to think: "Well here we go again then." I just couldn't be bothered with it. It was the constant being told what was the matter with her. I think everyone just wanted me to know that it was not my fault or anything.
>
> She was very, very focused on **her**, and kept needing reassurance that she was OK. It was always very 'about her'. But I guess it would be. It's understandable. But then, whenever she's been ill it's always felt like the biggest deal ever. She's always been a worrying kind of person. And then she used to keep asking me if I minded not doing stuff with her. She kept telling me, "It's because of the way I am at the moment". It was as if she was saying: "I don't want you to feel

> sorry for me, but I need to tell you this." I felt a bit offended really, because I thought that, as her sister, I shouldn't need to be told.
>
> It didn't affect me that badly really. I distanced myself because I felt that I couldn't do or say anything to help. If I talked to her I thought it would be more of a reason for her to talk about how she was instead of doing anything about it.

If you are particularly close to the person, you are likely to invest a great deal of time, attention and energy into helping them to manage and overcome their symptoms. This can be emotionally draining, especially if you are their main confidante. You therefore need to take great care to look after yourself so that you do not become exhausted and ill.

Dealing with someone who is overwhelmed by their symptoms can be tricky. It takes time and effort to do this effectively because it can feel as if you are bashing your head against a brick wall as their symptoms return again and again and again. No matter how much you feel for them, it can be challenging not to give in and scream: "For goodness sake – just snap out of it!" But they can't 'snap out of it'. If they could, they would.

What they need is to feel in control of themselves and to know that they will be OK. You need to have infinite patience in order to help them, and they need your support.

HOW TO HELP, NOT HINDER

Be informed

- Learn something of anxiety disorders and the symptoms a person might experience.
- If the person that is affected is someone you know well, find out all you can so that you can reinforce their understanding and reassure them.

- Understand that their symptoms form a constant background to their everyday life.

Calming tones, and choice of words

Mary, 20:

Mary telephoned home from college in a highly anxious state. Her father answered the phone. He was desperately concerned about her and wanted to help, but the words he used and the tone of his voice just made things worse. His utter frustration echoed through every second of the phone call.

"Look, just calm down. You'll have to calm down – I can't hear what you're saying. Why are you crying now? What's the matter? Oh my God, nothing seems to be working. You just seem to be surviving and you should be enjoying yourself. Nothing seems to be working."

Her father's words, combined with Mary's already high level of anxiety, raised her fear level to one of complete terror.

Petra, 40:

I get panic attacks. My husband doesn't understand them at all – he thinks I'm being over dramatic. It's awful. He had to drive me to the doctor last week I was so bad, and there I was with my head out the window and breathing into a paper bag, and he's frustrated and shouting at me:

"Stop it – just stop it. You're over-acting. Don't be so stupid." And my daughter was in the back crying. It was awful. Then when I got to the surgery, the doctor sort of talked me down, and I was all right then."

When someone is highly anxious, avoid saying:

Calm down
Stop it
Don't be stupid

Stop worrying
Snap out of it
Pull yourself together
Get a grip

There is something very unhelpful about being spoken to in this way. It feels as if you're being given an order. If you panic it will send the message of panic to them. So speak to the person in a calm, reassuring manner. Help them by using your voice effectively and saying the right things.

Your voice and the messages you give them:

- Keep your voice calm. This means avoiding letting your speech get faster and your voice become higher. They will pick up on any frustration and tension that you feel because it will show in your voice.
- Normalise everything they say. They feel bad enough as it is, so (whatever you might privately think) tell them that what they experience is quite normal in the circumstances and to be expected. This will help to reassure them.
- Be empathic. Imagine what the person must be going through, not how their anxiety is affecting you.
- Listen to what they are saying, even though they might be almost hysterical.
- Be careful of the words you use and what you say.
- Pick a few key statements that you can say when the person is experiencing their symptoms, such as: "It's OK. You know this is part of the process. It will pass."
- Always find something positive to say about how the person is coping, because this will encourage them. And always speak of the future in a positive and encouraging way.

- Know that by just 'being there' for the person – whether face to face or on the phone, you are doing more to help them than you might realise. They really need your support.

Put it in perspective and positive reframe

- Help the person to get things into perspective. If they are worrying and fretting about something specific, just calmly ask them:

  Well, can you do something about it?
  How important will this be to you in five years time?

- Help them to see the positive side to the issue or situation. Encourage them to look at it from a different angle. For example, if the person wants to avoid going into a shop in case they have an anxiety attack, you could point out that this would be a great opportunity to test out their ability to cope.
- Listen to the words they use, and help them to reframe their negative statements into positive ones, as in Chapter 1. Help them to take back control by changing the words they use.
- Always give them some positive feedback

Listen

- Really listen to what the person is saying. If you are with them, make eye contact – even if you find this tricky. A look of understanding and empathy from a person speaks volumes. It gives the message to someone who is suffering that you are there for them, and they are not alone. If you are on the other end of a telephone you've only got your voice, and the things that you say. Let them know that you are listening by making appropriate comments and assents, such as "Mmm …" occasionally. Keep your voice calm and reassuring – and avoid sighing. A sigh sends the message "I've had enough now," or "I'm bored."

- Think of yourself as a therapist. Always be listening for what lies under the surface of what the person tells you. They may be completely open and up-front to start with, but often there may be stories, and a period of skirting around the real issue. You may both find that talking is easier if you do an activity together, such as going for a walk, doing some exercise, or cooking.

Distract

- Distract them if you sense that it is appropriate to do so. For example, suggest that you do an activity together, that they make you a cup of tea, or just talk about something that interests them.
- Use humour. This can be a great distracter. I knew someone who was very worried about a presentation that she had to give at a job interview. After the interview she felt that she had gone to pieces and had done very badly. When she told her husband, he said in a very matter-of-fact way: "Well, at least you didn't fart!" She thought this was hilarious and felt much better about it all. Humour is great leveller. It helps to dissolve feelings of worry and anxiety. It also creates a sense of perspective and stops you thinking about the worst consequences.

Talk

- Talk to them. Help the person to challenge their limiting beliefs. They will be entrapped by them. They may not fully realise this, but much of their life will be all about survival – that is, how they can prevent themselves from feeling terrible. So they begin to see the world in a limiting way. Gently encourage them to see other possibilities. But take care not to make assumptions about what they want, and not to push them. The person must set their own agenda. They need to take back control. Also be aware that sometimes talking about situations which are uncomfortable for the person can trigger their symptoms again. But if this happens, you are there to help and reassure them.

- Help them to set specific and achievable goals, and encourage them to complete and achieve them.

- Help the person to feel good about themselves. Praise all achievements, no matter how small – especially where their progress in facing their fears is concerned. Remind them of their great personal qualities and of what they have achieved in the past. Their confidence will have taken a huge knock – remember, they may have thought that they were 'mad' or 'ill' – so your praise and encouragement will give them a boost.

- Encourage the person to ask for help.

"On the whole, women are much more easily able to do this than men. Usually the men are in a complete state by the time they come to us, because they've avoided acknowledging their feelings for so long. Eventually, they are forced to seek help, often by someone in the family." Dr Menzies Schrader, Associate Specialist Psychiatrist.

Many people are reluctant to ask for help for many reasons, and some just aren't sure how best to do it. Yet it's an important thing to be able to do in any situation. Asking for help takes away a certain amount of fear.

Clive, 43:
I was always nervous as a kid. I used to worry about my health and what people were thinking about me, and then I had agoraphobia between the ages of 19 and 26. It came on suddenly. I was terrified by open spaces. It just didn't make sense to me. I coped with it by staying indoors, so I was missing out on everything I should have been doing - having a 'normal' young guy's life like going out and having fun, and girlfriends and that. Well, I got some control back when I learnt to drive. I managed that, and in the end I cured myself because I used to drive somewhere and then make myself walk a certain distance to a destination. I increased the distance a little bit more each time until I could do it without thinking about it.

Looking back now though, I know the agoraphobia had a huge impact on my life. I'm sure it affected the way I think about things now. I know I'm a loner, and I'm more immature than most blokes of my age. And I am negative about things. I always find something negative to say about myself and put myself down a lot. I know I do that. I don't want to, and I wish I could stop, but ...

I guess I've always tried to live up to what other people expected of me. I remember once when I was a teenager, a friend of my mother's asked her if I had a girlfriend, and that really knocked me. She clearly thought I should have had one – and I hadn't. I don't really like being around other people much, even now, because I think that people are looking at me and judging me because I don't conform to the social 'norm'. I often think that people are talking about me and saying things behind my back.

Clive's sister:
Clive lives with my husband and me and he is a really kind and generous person. He's mild-mannered and thinks deeply about things. But I get so frustrated by him. I love him to bits because he's my little brother, but he drives me mad, and he knows how I feel.

For a start, he's the most negative man alive. He's got such low self-esteem. He constantly beats himself up about all the things he thinks he should be doing, or should have done. He criticises himself so much – yet he does nothing to sort himself out. He comes across to us as if he's just absorbed in himself all the time - as if everything's about how it affects **him** and no one else. OK, he did have a rough time when he was younger with his agoraphobia, but he's always had good family support. He's still anxious and gets far too worried about things, and he's so negative generally. I think this makes him 'blinkered' when it comes to other people - he has very strong views and opinions, and sometimes he says what he thinks without ever considering how he might upset someone.

He moans about his job all the time and I suppose, all credit to him, he did send off for details about another one. But as soon as the application form came, he took one look at the person specification and tore it up because he assumed he didn't have enough of the qualifications they'd marked as 'essential'. It was ridiculous – he didn't even read the whole thing, and I know he would have stood a good chance of an interview.

I wish he'd get some counselling or something because I think he is never going to be happy while he's like this. Whenever we mention it, he gets angry and insists he can do it all himself. He says: "I bought a car and cured myself of agoraphobia," but I can't help feeling it could take for ever. I mean, he's still quite young really and could have a great life, but he has to do something to make it happen.

HOW MUCH TO GIVE AND FOR HOW LONG

This is tricky. There is no doubt that the person needs support and understanding and, in many ways, they may need you to lead them gently, or to work alongside them. But then you will need to withdraw for their own good. So for you, the time in between is a period of 'watchful waiting'. You will make a judgement and decide when and how back off.

I would always say that if you have a choice between doing what is right and doing what is kind, do what is kind – but sensibly. If you are not careful, there is a danger that your unconditional support and help enables the anxiety to continue. For a time, the individual needs all the support and reassurance they can get. But later on, if they are continually wanting you to reassure them, they are not learning. They are using you as a crutch. It can get to a point where the individual gets comfort out of having someone tell them what to do, so a dependency develops. But what they really need to do is understand that they can be in control. So when a trusted person withdraws their support, the individual may think that they don't want to help them – whereas really what that person is doing is helping them to become confident in their own ability.

So avoid making decisions for an adult who has an anxiety disorder, even though they may want you to. If you do, you disempower them.

However, there is a fine line between giving too much support and too little. Beware of withdrawing too much support, and too soon. Some would say that people never learn if they are not made to fend for themselves, and that to do so is 'character building' – especially if someone is young. But in my view you can have too much 'character building'. Tough love does not *always* work. It can tip a person over the edge.

The following is Annie's story. It is also her mother's.

> **Annie, 24:**
> Just before Christmas I'd been sick and fainted at university, and it was the whole thing of feeling scared that it might happen again while I was away from home. I think it planted a memory there really. I wasn't happy in halls anyway, and I actually found I got very homesick. I became really sensitive to noise and couldn't sleep properly, and I just found that I was, well – just frightened really. I found sitting through lectures difficult because I felt panicky, and I had to leave the job I had for the same reason. I panicked when I travelled on the Tube. Everything seemed to intensify, and I stopped doing things with my friends. I didn't tell many people how I felt though.
>
> **Annie's mum:**
> We'd get frantic phone calls at all sorts of times. Sometimes she'd be hysterical. Once she had made a supreme effort to go and see some friends. She'd got on the bus and just panicked. She phoned up weeping, saying she didn't know what to do and she was so

scared of everything. She said her mind was churning and she couldn't stop herself thinking. She was scared that she was going mad. I spent most of her journey trying to calm her down over the phone and reassure her. I felt so helpless. Then we lost contact when she got off the bus.

About 15 minutes later I phoned her to see if she was OK and she said she was a bit better – a friend had met her and kept talking to her to keep her mind off how she was feeling.

I rang again about half an hour later because I was worried, and she sounded OK.

She came home at Christmas and I wasn't certain that she would be able to go back. On Christmas Eve she said she'd spent the whole night with her stomach feeling as if it was taking a sharp intake of breath. She said it was a feeling of "something's going to happen", and she said she felt nervous and anxious, as if everything was coming to a head. She described being overwhelmed by everything she has to do, and too tired; in fact she said, "My soul is tired." She kept feeling sick and scared and saying, "I'm scared of everything."

At one stage Annie was texting me very frequently throughout the day to tell me exactly how she felt, and finishing each text with "Do you think that's normal?" She just wanted constant reassurance. To be honest, my heart used to sink because I knew that most times a text from Annie would mean that something was wrong, and there was a limit to what I could say. These are some of the messages:

I can't relax and my heart will not stop beating fast. I keep being jolted awake by feelings of panic. No matter what I do I'm tense.

Feel detached from everything. Think I'm going crazy.

If you have time tonight could you phone me?

Felt like I was really going to faint for a couple of secs in the night but was OK. I know it sounds silly but I dread this feeling, and can't believe I am making something so physical happen. I am scared of it happening when I'm not at home as it feels so horrible. I just feel like I have no control over it at all.

Am in a lecture. Have just had seminar, but the lecture is harder as my mind wanders and I'm sure my energy is low and I'm going to faint or be sick.

The sick feeling's come back again.

Just now I can't sleep. I feel too sick.

Could you phone me. I just want to talk to someone.

Somehow managed to get through my lecture. First half was absolute agony. I'm not having fun.

Had an OK day. Once again managed to get to lecture even though didn't feel like it.

Don't know how I'm doing it. Am still all up and down. I hope I'm dealing with this the best way. It's so scary.

I can't take this any more, the feelings are too scary.

I feel almost permanently miserable and don't know what to do with myself.

I took to keeping my mobile by the bed, just in case. It was a bit like having a new baby again – I'd wake up at every 'bleep'.

It was awful. The whole experience was dreadful for Annie and it was emotionally draining for me. It was worrying for the whole family, but I was the one she talked to most because she knew that I understood how she felt. I know that you have to be careful about not doing too much for someone, but a person in that situation needs as much support as they can get because they feel so alone, and they need to feel they're understood.

Actually, I was given some good advice from a friend who's a psychologist. He said that living away from home was probably tougher than she'd realised (even though she'd been away many times before), and that anything could have just triggered something in her. He said that she was the only one who would really be able to get herself out of this. He thought we should stand back a bit, but be there for her. He also suggested that I save up the texts until the end of the day – for my own sanity – but to tell her, so that she wouldn't be too alarmed. I did this, but felt awkward not answering the texts straight away. But often by the time I replied she was feeling quite different anyway.

Amazingly, I found I **was** able to stand back a bit. That really helped me, because the whole thing was really getting me down. I just felt sure that she would be OK and that she would get through this.

Annie:
I went back to uni, and I had Cognitive Behavioural Therapy while I was there. That was quite useful. It helped me to manage, but the feelings were still there. I began to see things differently. For example, I felt really strongly sick in the morning when I woke up, but I understood that really this was all in my head – that my fears were creating this physical thing. Sometimes I'd retch, but I could stop myself when I forced myself to think of other things.

I stopped feeling panicky on the Tube, but it was just this crippling sickness. Every day. It was horrible. All I'd want to do was curl up in bed for about 10 minutes. It did only last for about five to 10 minutes at a time.

I had talked to my tutor about having time out from my degree but he said it would be better not to if I could help it. So I chose modules for the rest of it, which meant that I could research on my own

> a lot and do the minimum of lectures. This meant that I could spend a lot of time at home and only go to London when I needed to. I just wanted some tranquillity again. I know it might seem like this was avoiding things, but it was the only way for me to get through, and in the end I came out with a good degree.
>
> Now that I'm better I know I did the right thing for me. I work in London now, but I go home at weekends because I know I don't ever want to live in London full-time again. I love London – I just don't want to live there. Some of my friends don't understand this at all, but I know it's the way I need to be – for me. I've learnt that.
>
> I've noticed that each year I always feel really sick some days just before Christmas. Then I wonder if all the old feelings will come back again. It's strange how it always happens at the same time as when it first did at uni. That was just before Christmas. But now I remind myself that it's just a memory of how it used to be, and I dismiss it. I know it will go eventually.

The experience of anxiety disorder gives a person a process through which to develop and strengthen. It is essential to their recovery that you both acknowledge this, and look to the future in a positive way.

Paula's sister experienced GAD for some time. She talked to Paula and her other sister about how she felt and looked to them both for reassurance. But she confided in her other sister more, and tended to go to her first. Though Paula was always willing to help, she made the following observation, which I think is useful.

> **Paula:**
> Just be there for that person but if they've already got one person they can really talk to, that's enough, so stand back a bit. To have more people to talk to about how they feel gives them more reason to talk about it, and I'm not sure that's helpful. Maybe it helps to reinforce their anxiety in their own minds.

But you can encourage them to listen to others. Someone might just say the right thing at the right time that rings true for the person and sets them on the road to recovery.

The right word, said at the right time can set you free

Chapter 13

How to look after yourself when you care for somone who has an anxiety disorder

"Crippling depression and chronic anxiety are the biggest causes of misery in Britain today. They are the great submerged problem, which shame keeps out of sight. But if you mention them, you soon discover how many families are affected. According to the respected Psychiatric Morbidity Survey, one in six of us would be diagnosed as having depression or chronic anxiety disorder, which means that one family in three is affected."

Professor Lord Richard Layard

The Depression Report - A New Deal for Depression and Anxiety Disorders http://cep.info@lse.ac.uk/textonly/research/mentalhealth/DEPRESSION_REPORT_LAYARD.pdf published June 2006 by The Centre for Economic Performance, London School of Economics and Political Science (cep.info@lse.ac.uk.)

HOW TO LOOK AFTER YOURSELF WHEN YOU CARE FOR SOMEONE WHO HAS AN ANXIETY DISORDER

Worry, anxiety and negative thoughts and feelings can eat away at you and gobble up your inner strength and resources. There is a very real danger that this could happen to you as you support someone through an anxiety disorder. You are likely to experience a whole range of thoughts and emotions as you do your best to help the person, and this can drag you down.

So you need to protect yourself against this and take care of yourself in order to keep mentally strong and healthy – for your own benefit and for theirs. It's so tough to see someone you love in distress, and the help you can give is limited. Ultimately, the individual has to take control themselves. You can only be there for them and do what you can. But you cannot afford to let them suck you dry, and the more they need you, the more your inner energy will be depleted. So you need to take steps to make sure that you are OK. You have to think of yourself as a separate package really, and learn to distance yourself emotionally, whilst remaining compassionate.

Be mindful of the fact that your own feelings and fears for the person could transfer to them. You may well be thinking: "When are they ever going to get out of this state?" or "I'm not sure that they'll ever be able to cope on their own again" If they get the slightest notion that you think this way, they will latch on to it, absorb it and it will increase and reinforce their own anxiety and doubts. Equally, you may absorb what *they* think and feel (reinforced by the number of times they will tell you) so much that it actually becomes what you think too.

You will benefit from doing many of the things in Chapter 11 to keep yourself calm and strong. In addition, the following will be useful for you:

Understand that their anxiety disorder is not under your control. You may not be able to change a person's behaviour but you do have a choice about how you deal with your own thoughts and feelings. This can be really challenging, but you *do* have a choice. (See Chapter 1)

- Avoid blaming yourself, especially if it is your child that is affected by anxiety disorder. Even if they are now adult, you probably still feel a sense of responsibility for them. And this can go hand in hand with feelings of guilt. For example, you may ask yourself why they suffer so much, and how perhaps you could have done something differently in the past. You long for them to be happy.

Brigitte:

I'm always there for my son. We sit and talk about his anxiety sometimes but I feel powerless to help him. Even though I've been through this myself, I can't do anything to take away his pain. I wish I could. All I can do is be there for him.

And that's the great thing. You *can* be there – in person, or on the phone. Avoid feeling guilty because it's pointless. What good can it possibly do? Think about how to help the person move forward in their life instead. Taking positive action will be of far more use to them, and to you.

- Accept that you may not be able to provide answers, but you can help the person to find a place of mental peace.
- Accept that you have feelings and express them somehow. Avoid bottling them up.
- You too need support. Their anxiety disorder is bewildering for you too. Talk to someone else about how you feel, even if you have been sworn to secrecy. This is not about going against someone's wishes – it is common sense, and necessary for your own health and wellbeing. There are many people you can talk to in absolute confidence, such as your doctor or a private therapist. Also, make use of the excellent telephone mental health helplines that are available. The person on the other end will listen and, if appropriate, provide advice. Some organisations provide email support, which many people find helpful too.

Radley:

The worst thing was that I had no support. My wife asked me not to tell anyone about her anxiety attacks, so I didn't – out of respect for

> her. But I wish I had, because it was a terrible time and I didn't know how to deal with it.

- Imagine some sort of protective covering around you all the time, like a personal protection insurance, to keep you mentally safe. You never quite know when the person who has the anxiety disorder will want your undivided time, attention and energy. Without meaning to, they can chip away at your inner resources until there seems to be nothing left. You might like to imagine being inside a bubble, or surrounded by a light, or to wear an imaginary cloak that covers you completely. This will help to put some distance between you, which is vital to your wellbeing. This can be easier said than done, but it's worth working at it.
- Do things that you enjoy, that are just for yourself.
- Take time to relax. An activity such as yoga, tai chi, or the Alexander Technique can really help you to de-stress, and this is so important because it is the build-up of stress that does the damage. One of the other benefits of this kind of activity is that you gradually become aware of where and how you carry tension in your body – and once you are aware, you can do something about it. You might also like to use the progressive relaxation technique outlined in Chapter 11.
- Keep a sense of perspective. Many others are going through a similar experience, so you are not alone.
- Be selfish, but with compassion and with a conscience. Accept that you can only do the best that you can. The affected person needs to know that you are there, but ultimately this is a path that they have to travel alone.
- Think positive and maintain a sense of fun.
- Understand that tough love doesn't necessarily work.
- Expect nothing in return.

Chapter 14

How to build up your confidence

The experience of an anxiety disorder knocks your confidence. There's no doubt about that. Well, the good news is that confidence can grow. You might just need a few tools to help you along the way.

- **Set yourself some clear objectives**

  Ask yourself what you are aiming for and what you want to happen. Once you are clear about this, you can start to think about how you might get there. Make sure your objectives are very specific and something that you know you will be able to do. Give yourself a time or a date to work towards. When you've done it, be really pleased. Every accomplishment is one step towards having greater confidence in your own ability.

  If you do not accomplish what you set out to do – no matter. Avoid beating yourself up about it. You'll do it next time.

- **Make a decision and stick to it.**

  Even if you decide to do nothing, let it be your choice, and your decision. Best to take charge and be firm about this, so that you accept responsibility and take control, otherwise you may feel that things 'just happen' to you.

  If the outcome is not what you expect – no matter. You made a decision, and that in itself is important because taking that step empowers you.

- **Ask for help**

  It is absolutely fine to ask for help if you need it. You may feel awkward about this, and in fact many people do. So if you are apprehensive about doing this, here are some simple steps to follow to make it easier:

  - Be specific about what you want help with.
  - Choose the best person to help you.
  - Decide how, when and where you are going to ask them, and what you will say.
  - Do it.

- **Be assertive**

  Being assertive involves stating what you want, clearly, politely and confidently. Ideally both you and the other person should feel satisfied with the outcome. Follow these three steps to stand the best chance of getting what you want:

  - State what the situation is.
  - Say how you feel about it.
  - Say what you want to happen and how this will benefit you both.

- **Keep a sense of perspective**

  Remember that many others feel just as you do now, so you are not alone.

  Accept that in the fullness of time, you *will* feel better. You will grow and develop from your experience and probably discover amazing qualities that you never knew you had.

Chapter 15

Useful lessons learnt

The vast majority of people that I spoke to for this book felt that they had actually benefited in some way from going through their experience of anxiety disorder. I think this is the amazing thing about it – you can go through such torment yet come out of it a stronger person, and often with a rather different, and perhaps healthier, perspective on life. The following four people are sparkling examples of this:

> **Steve:**
> It doesn't matter if I'm not in control of everything. I've realised that I don't have to control **everything**. It doesn't matter if I let some things go. I don't have to be in control all the time. I have much more fun now that I realise that.
>
> **Marie:**
> I used to think, "I must do this" and "I should be doing that". All the time, putting unnecessary pressure on myself. I was aware that everyone around me was stressed – working stupidly long hours, and it was relentless. They had no life outside work except for a quick trip to the pub. I started to realise that you don't have to live like that. You just don't have to live your life like that.
>
> **Kim:**
> Whenever I feel that things could get on top of me now, I tell myself,

"It doesn't matter. It really **doesn't** matter." I just keep quietly saying it inside until it sticks. It really helps, you know.

Julie:

I'm very organised. And at one time I'd have even had to know what I was going to eat and when, or I'd have been anxious about it. Now I just let it happen more. It's been a good lesson.

The following is a summary of the advice that people wanted to pass on to others:

- It's important to be honest with yourself and others.
- Never be ashamed to ask for help.
- Thousands of people have been there before you and many, many of them have got through it.
- Make it easy on yourself – it's OK to do whatever gets you through.
- Tell people what's going on for you, because several of them will turn out to have been through it themselves and they'll be a huge support to you.
- Understand that you **will** feel better and that it's only temporary. Accept what's happening to you.
- Look into various treatments.
- Don't listen to people who tell you what you should and shouldn't be doing.
- Avoid setting yourself stupidly high standards in general – things that you feel you should do and live up to.
- Don't beat yourself up for feeling the way you do.
- Speak to people about how you feel. People are more supportive than you think.

- Know that just because what you experience is ghastly, intense and frightening, it is **not** the end of the world.

This is all *great* advice. I think it's wonderful that people want to share their experiences to help each other. So take strength from the fact that you are definitely not alone. Others have gone through similar experiences to you. There is always someone, somewhere who understands what you are going through and who can help you – if you'll let them.

Know that you will feel good again and that you will probably be stronger and wiser than you have ever been. So look forward to your future, and be ready to enjoy it. You absolutely deserve it.

Useful contacts

You'll also find this list on our website at www.whiteladderpress.com where you can click through on the links.

MENTAL HEALTH CONTACTS AND HELPLINES

Samaritans
www.samaritans.org
24-hour helpline 08457 90 90 90

NHS Direct
www.nhsdirect.nhs.uk
24-hour helpline 0845 46 47

Sane
www.sane.org.uk
020 7375 1002

SANEline (helpline) 0845 767 8000

SANEmail (provides email support) sanemail@sane.org.uk

National Phobics Society
www.phobics-society.org.uk
08444 775 774
The largest charity dealing with anxiety disorders

MIND
www.mind.org.uk
0845 766 0163
Provides a range of information and leaflets on all aspects of mental health

First Steps to Freedom
www.first-steps.org
Helpline 0845 120 2916
For all anxiety and phobia issues

No Panic
www.nopanic.org.uk
Helpline 10am-10pm every day of the year
0808 808 0545
Support for suffers of anxiety disorders

Anxiety Care
www.anxietycare.org.uk
Helpline 0208 478 3400
Masses of information on anxiety disorders

The Mental Health Foundation
www.mentalhealth.org.uk
020 7803 1101
No helpline, but lots of useful information from this charity

The Depression Alliance
www.depressionalliance.org
0845 123 23 20
The leading UK charity for those affected by depression

FOR CARERS:

Carers UK
www.carersuk.org
020 7922 800
CarersLine (helpline) 0808 808 7777

INFORMATION ON THERAPIES AND PRACTITIONER REGISTERS

British Association for Counselling and Psychotherapy (BACP)
www.bacp.co.uk
0870 443 5252

United Kingdom Council for Psychotherapy (UKCP)
www.psychotherapy.org.uk
020 7014 9955

Homeopathy

Alliance of Registered Homeopaths
www.a-r-h.org
08700 736339

Society of Homeopaths
www.homeopathy-soh.org
0845 450 6611

Acupuncture

British Acupuncture Council
www.acupuncture.org.uk
020 8735 0400

Hypnotherapy

General Hypnotherapy Register
www.general-hypnotherapy-register.com
01590 683770

Also see the General Hypnotherapy Standards Council
www.ghsc.co.uk

Neuro-Linguistic Programming (NLP)

Association for Neuro-Linguistic Programming
www.anlp.org
0845 053 1162

Practitioners also listed on www.general-hpnotherapy-register.com
01590 683770

Nutrition

The British Association of Nutritional Therapists (BANT)
www.bant.org.uk
08706 061284

The Institute for Optimum Nutrition
www.ion.ac.uk
020 8614 7800

The Alexander Technique

The Society of Teachers of Alexander Technique
www.stat.org.uk
0845 230 7878
A great way to relieve stress